MEN AND WOMEN
WHO MAKE MUSIC

BOOKS BY DAVID EWEN

THE UNFINISHED SYMPHONY

FROM BACH TO STRAVINSKY

WINE, WOMEN AND WALTZ

THE MAN WITH THE BATON

COMPOSERS OF TODAY

HEBREW MUSIC

COMPOSERS OF YESTERDAY

TWENTIETH CENTURY COMPOSERS

MUSICAL VIENNA
(*In collaboration with Dr. Frederic Ewen*)

Paderewski's Hands

Fritz Kreisler

MEN
and WOMEN
Who Make
MUSIC

By DAVID EWEN

THOMAS · Y · CROWELL COMPANY

New York : 1939

To the Memory of
LEOPOLD GODOWSKY

PREFACE

IT HAS been often said that the musical interpreter is the connecting link—the catalytic agent, so to speak—between great music and the audience. Through the interpreter's virtuosity, through his scholarly comprehension of the composer's intentions, through the vibrancy of his personality and his power of recreation, he projects for the sensitive listener the aesthetic experiences he has found in the masterpieces of music. Thus, the art of the interpreter is as infinitely varied as the number of interpreters: Each one brings to a work of art his individual personality and background, which give it its shape and form and subtleties of expression. Thus, too, the art of interpretation will always hold for the music lover a singular and inexhaustible fascination.

This book portrays fifteen great interpreters of music who enrich so immeasurably the life of music-lovers in this country. With the exception of one, these interpreters are at the present time the bone and marrow of musical life in America. While it had been my original intention to confine this book only to those interpreters who are now actively engaged in concert work in this country, it was unthinkable for me to prepare a book on virtuosos which would omit an artist of the stature of Pablo

vii

Casals, who has not visited here for so many years. Not that there are no omissions in this book!—omissions of great artists who are also an integral part of our concert experiences, artists (to choose some names at random) like Emanuel Feuermann, Efrem Zimbalist, Friedrich Schorr, Myra Hess, Marian Anderson, Rudolf Serkin, Bruno Walter, etc. But because the interpretative art is so rich, it is impossible to include *everybody* of importance—impossible and, it should be added, undesirable. For the repetitiousness of the material would have merely invited boredom.

I have, therefore, decided to include no more than fifteen virtuosos—those fifteen who might best represent a cross-section of present-day musical interpretation, those fifteen in whom the American concertgoer might be most interested.

It has been a long time since a book on interpreters has made an appearance, either in this country or in Europe; so long a time, as a matter of fact, that at least ten of these fifteen artists are here being treated within the covers of a book for the first time. Many kind readers, who enjoyed my previous books on great orchestral conductors [1] and great modern composers,[2] have written asking me to consider a similar treatment for great con-

---

[1] *The Man With the Baton*, Thomas Y. Crowell Co., 1936.
[2] *Twentieth Century Composers*, Thomas Y. Crowell Co., 1937.

cert artists. I yielded to their wish because I, too, felt that the absence of a recent book on great musical interpreters was a serious gap in musical literature.

The treatment in this book is similar to that adopted in my last work, *Twentieth Century Composers*. The attempt is to give the layman a more intimate understanding of the virtuoso art "from the point of view most easily assimilated and understood; that of the personalities themselves who have given shape and direction to music." As in *Twentieth Century Composers*, the emphasis in this book is on "biographical and personal material: the biographical material enabling the reader to understand the background and circumstances which inspired the musician, and the personal material giving the reader an intimate introduction to those personalities that gave voice to this music. . . . Critical appraisal, however, is not sacrificed."

With the exception of three chapters, the virtuosos themselves have supplied the biographical and personal material for these studies, and then carefully checked up on the accuracy of the material. Thus, the material in this book—with three exceptions—is first-hand, drawn from many personal meetings, conversations and social contacts with the musicians themselves. For their patience and whole-hearted cooperation, I should like here to express my profound indebtedness.

CONTENTS

ILLUSTRATIONS

MEN AND WOMEN WHO MAKE MUSIC

I: KREISLER

CHAPTER ONE

FRITZ KREISLER

FATE being what it is, it is not beyond the realm of possibility that the name of Fritz Kreisler will descend to posterity for a reason other than that he has been one of the greatest violinists of our age. One can almost foresee some musical dictionary of the twenty-first century referring to Kreisler in this fashion: "He was one of the most distinguished artists of his generation, and a composer of many delightful morsels for his instrument. He is remembered today only because of a hoax which he perpetrated on the entire world of music in his time, presenting his own compositions as products of such masters as Vivaldi, Martini, Couperin, Pugnani, Francoeur, etc. For more than thirty years, this hoax went undetected, until the composer himself revealed the truth."

Yet, as Kreisler himself has confessed to his close friends, he had no intention of pulling the nose of the music world.When, many years ago, he presented his "transcriptions"—with the fabulous explanation that he had stumbled across the original manuscripts in European monasteries and had freely adapted them for the

3

violin—it was not to test the critical acumen of his fellow musicians but merely as a temporary, though ethically questionable, expedient of a young and unknown violinist who wished to have his own works performed more widely. However, with the deception far more successful than Kreisler ever dared to hope, he discovered that it was not quite so easy to confess to the world that he had quietly palmed off a fraud. He, therefore, nursed his secret, always alert for some propitious moment in which to relieve himself of it gracefully.

The moment arrived a few years ago when the distinguished New York music critic, Olin Downes, attempted to trace the source of Pugnani's *Praeludium and Allegro*. He communicated first with Kreisler's publishers, and then with Kreisler himself. He was told unequivocally, and without the slightest attempt at subterfuge on the part of the violinist, that the piece was original; that, as a matter of fact, the majority of the other so-called "transcriptions" were original as well. And one could almost sense a sigh of infinite relief accompanying the confession.

It was to be expected that musicians and critics should greet the hoax as if it were a personal offense, with grumbles of anger and denunciations of Kreisler's "artistic dishonesty." A scattered few met the confession with what Kreisler described as "good humor and splendid sportsmanship." But, for the most part, Kreisler was treated with scathing criticism. "We wish to apply the term discreditable to the whole transaction from start to finish," commented one eminent music journal editorially. Some critics, headed by Ernest Newman, flayed Kreisler with merciless lashes of their verbal whips. The music world felt somewhat silly and not a little awkward and embarrassed to learn that it had been a victim of a fraud for which all of musical history can find no counterpart. There have been composers who have concealed their identities under manufactured pseudonyms. But never before this has a composer masqueraded his music behind the great names of the past, to have the music accepted as genuine without question or suspicion. "It is as though Mr. Yeats published poems under the name of Herrick or Spenser," pointed out Ernest Newman.

Yet studying the entire affair in retrospect, musicians should not have been taken altogether by surprise. Twenty years ago, Kreisler presented his *Liebesfreud*, *Liebesleid* and *Schön Rosmarin* as "transcriptions" of posthumous pieces by Josef Lanner. It was only because a Viennese critic assailed Kreisler for his impudence in including his own *Caprice Viennois* in the same group with "these gems of Lanner" that Kreisler indignantly confessed that these pieces were actually his own and not Lanner's. This episode might have passed without much publicity at the time, but musicians were well acquainted with it and often made reference to it. One would, therefore, expect that Kreisler's other transcriptions would have been subjected to a more rigorous scrutiny. Particularly since a warning flashed from the frontispiece of every Kreisler publication: "The original manuscripts used for these transcriptions are the private property of Mr. Fritz Kreisler and are now published for the first time; they are, moreover, so freely treated that *they constitute, in fact, original works*." The italics are mine; but they might easily have been Kreisler's.

Perhaps some musicians suspected the authenticity of this music. It may have been only because the fraud was much too perfect that the world permitted itself to be duped for so long a time.

It is very doubtful, however, if Kreisler's confession has diminished to a perceptible degree his enormous stature in the eyes of his audience. Few artists of our time —with the possible exceptions of Toscanini and Paderewski—have inspired such adoration from audiences throughout the world as Kreisler has since 1900. An adoration such as this is not so easily dissipated. Even when the incident was fresh in the minds of the music public, the feeling was strong among many of them that the deception was, after all, nothing worse than a youthful indiscretion, and that Kreisler later handled the very difficult situation of making an open confession with fearless honesty. And the unquestionable skill with which Kreisler mimicked the style of the old masters could not fail to elicit a certain measure of well-deserved admiration.

In any case, Kreisler's singular fascination for his audience was in no great danger. With the first unpleasantness and bitterness forgotten, the incident even brought him additional glory.

2

The enormous attraction that Kreisler holds for his audiences arises not merely from the magic of violin and bow, but also from his unique personal charm. The poise and refinement of his platform manner, the dignity and yet cordial warmth of his relationship with his audience, have an appeal the strength of which cannot be questioned. His soft smile, in response to an ovation, is of ineffable sweetness, and his eyes are warm and kind. He possesses to an unusual degree the ability to create at his concerts an intimacy and personal contact between himself and his audience, which succeed in making even the largest concert hall assume the friendliness of a small drawing-room.

For a long time now, Kreisler's personality has been

7

touched with glamour in the eyes of his audience. His intense humanity and great heart have, probably, inspired as much admiration as his sublime playing. His activities during and after the World War, for example. It need not be retold in detail that he sent a large proportion of his earnings to Austria to help alleviate the terrible suffering and despair of his fellow countrymen during the post-War period. It is said that Mrs. Kreisler personally interested herself in the future of forty-two orphans, because she had promised their dying fathers in the hospital to look after them. And Kreisler was directly responsible for the support of some fifteen hundred starving artists. All of Kreisler's earnings, for a period of more than five years, flowed into Austria, where his wife contributed her marvelous energy and devotion in dividing the money among the sick, the starving and the crushed. His devotion to charitable work during these years was so great that everything else pertaining to his art and life assumed secondary importance.

Ernö Balogh, who for a short time was Kreisler's accompanist, told me an anecdote which is particularly illuminating in giving us an insight into a great character. Shortly after the War, while concertizing in Norway, Kreisler was invited to have tea with the King—an honor which most artists would have accepted with unmitigated delight. Kreisler, however, apologized for not coming, explaining that he was too busy. That afternoon, Kreisler remained in his hotel to do secretarial work for a series of charities which he was conducting for needy Europeans. "But," Balogh said to him with surprise, "you told His Majesty that you were too busy to have tea with him, and now you are doing only charity work!" "Charity work—that is something else," Kreisler answered softly. "Why should I go out of my way to have tea with a king? With a great thinker or humanitarian—yes, I would gladly spend precious time with such a man. But a king? No, thank you. It's much more important to spend the time in helping these poor starving people!"

"And that," added Balogh as a commentary, "is a characteristic Kreisler gesture."

Such human generosity could not, of course, fail to make Kreisler a singularly appealing figure. Equally important in inspiring the admiration of his public is his wit, spontaneous and pointed, which has frequently been quoted and repeated in music circles. One story is well-known: at one time a Chicago heiress invited him to give a performance at a private party she was giving, and inquired his fee. "Three thousand dollars," Kreisler told her. "The fee, Mr. Keisler, is satisfactory. But, of course, you realize that you are not to mingle with the guests." "In that case," answered Kreisler, "the fee is only two thousand."

What has aroused most adulation among music audiences has been Kreisler's profound cultural background, which is quite unique among musicians. His many talents, which branch out into so many diverse directions, have long been subject for discussion and awe among concertgoers.

He is almost as gifted with piano as with violin; and now it is more apparent than ever before that his creative talent is not much less significant than his interpretative. He can paint with a sure and tasteful brush. Early in his life he studied in the famous atelier of Julien in Paris, where he revealed such great promise that it seemed that art and not music would become his life work. He is well schooled in mathematics and the sciences, and has a very intimate acquaintance with medicine. His linguistic talents are enormous. Not merely is he able to speak eight languages with fluency and possesses a solid foundation of Greek and Latin, but he is also a devoted student of philology, of which he has made an intensive study. He is a lover of books—a famous collector, as a matter of fact; and he has an admirable literary background. His fine critical sense is the result of an intellectual background that embraces philosophy, logic and metaphysics. Obviously, he has been fed on a well balanced cultural diet, and his appetite has been so keen that he has been able to take more than a mere superficial taste of each

dish. The result has been a fertile background of scholarship which for ever so long has made him a personality
to admire and respect.

3

It is this enormous culture that is reflected in his violin-
playing and gives it a great part of its individuality and
character. With age, Kreisler's technique may falter and
his tone may become diluted; but his phrasing, his dynamics and his deftly superimposed nuances—fruits of
his maturity and wisdom—are the unmistakable finger-
prints on his performances, and are familiar to anyone
who has heard him play.

Almost any violinist—not excluding even Heifetz or
Menuhin—will sound like any other half-dozen great
violinists in playing certain small pieces. Kreisler, however, is unable to play twelve bars of music without dis-
closing himself. In this connection, I am reminded of a
story which Kreisler likes so well to tell, and which is
indicative of the way in which the entire world is familiar
with his style.

Kreisler was browsing in an antique shop in Antwerp
when he came upon a cheap violin. He called the pawnbroker to him—"an old Jew who seemed to have stepped
out of a picture of Rembrandt," as Kreisler himself de-

scribed him—and asked the price. Then, somewhat playfully, he took his own violin out of the case and asked the old Jew if he would care to purchase it. The old Jew looked at the violin, handled it with careful fingers, and then said: "I am afraid that I am not rich enough to pay you what the violin is worth." Then, as though in afterthought, the pawnbroker added: "Would you please wait here two minutes? I'll dash home and bring you an Amati violin which will certainly interest you." In a few minutes he returned—with a policeman. "That man," the Jew cried, pointing a crooked finger at the somewhat bewildered violinist, "is a thief. Arrest him! He has in his possession a violin belonging to Fritz Kreisler!"

In vain did Kreisler protest that he himself was the great violinist; the fact that he had left his passport in his hotel room did not simplify the situation. Finally, Kreisler put the violin under his chin and played *Schön Rosmarin*. "There's no doubt about it," the pawnbroker said with a voice that cracked with bewilderment. "This gentleman simply can't be anyone else but Fritz Kreisler!"

What distinguishes Kreisler's playing from that of so many other violinists is not merely a profound culture which brings new significance to every phrase or accent. Nor does it lie in technique. A dissection of Kreisler's playing might focus attention on the warmth and humanity of his tone, the resilience of his bow in *spiccato* passages, or the incomparable grace of his trill; but these are not entirely adequate in explaining the true nature of Kreisler's art. It is rather an indefinable quality which is sometimes vaguely described as the "Kreisler charm." To explain Kreisler's violin most felicitously, it is necessary to borrow the characterization which for centuries has been applied to the city of Kreisler's birth, Vienna— namely, *Gemütlichkeit*. Kreisler's violin-playing is essentially Viennese in its grace, fullness of heart, zest for life. It is the embodiment of the Viennese spirit of the Schubert *Ländler,* the waltzes of Lanner and Johann Strauss, the operettas of Franz Lehár. His art is Viennese in its subtle refinement and intriguing sparkle of personality.

For two centuries the Viennese people have had a felicitous word with which to describe life in the Austrian capital. That word, *flott*—implying zest and buoyancy— might most aptly describe the violin-playing of Fritz Kreisler.

4

Legend would have us believe that Fritz Kreisler was driven by an uncontrollable force to music and the violin from his earliest years. The truth, however, is that as a child Kreisler detested the playing of the violin and that throughout his entire career he periodically attempted to escape from his instrument.

He was born in Vienna on February 2, 1875, and was given his first lessons on the violin by his father, an eminent Viennese physician and icthyologist. It was only with the greatest of difficulty that his father could bring the boy to practise his exercises; he persisted in his demands that the boy study the violin assiduously only because Fritz disclosed such extraordinary talent from the very first. At the age of seven, Fritz Kreisler made his public début, playing several small pieces for the violin on a program featuring Carlotta Patti (sister of the immortal Adelina). His taste and musicianship were both apparent, and it was decided to enroll him in the Vienna Conservatory for an intensive course of music study. Despite the fact that the minimum age requirement for the Vienna Conservatory was fourteen, Fritz Kreisler, aged seven, was immediately admitted. After three years of study under Joseph Hellmesberger (one of the most famous Viennese musicians of the time, and something of the city's musical legislator), Kreisler received the gold medal for violin-playing. During these years of study his musical tastes were given permanent shape by performances he heard given by Joseph Joachim and Anton Rubinstein—performances which he has never forgotten.

From Vienna he went to Paris, where he was admitted

to the Paris Conservatory, a pupil of Massart in violin-playing and Delibes in theory. Once again Kreisler astounded his professors, this time by winning the *Premier Grand Prix* for violin-playing in his twelfth year, in a competition in which every entrant was about ten years his senior. However, the practising of exercises was, as Kreisler today confesses, always an ordeal for him; it was only with the greatest of reluctance that he would pick up violin and bow for his daily study. Even many years later, at the height of his career, Kreisler reduced his practising to a minimum, far below the number of hours which other violinists require to keep their fingers agile.

It is incorrect to believe that Kreisler's artistic path has been one of glory from the first. When, in 1888, he came to America on his first concert tour in a series of joint recitals with Moriz Rosenthal, the pianist, (Kreisler was then only fourteen years old), he played charmingly enough to receive a few kind notices from the critics; but to call his American début sensational would be to stretch the truth to a point of exaggeration. As a matter of fact, his talent was so calmly accepted that, when he returned to Vienna shortly thereafter, he was found unsuitable even for a position as second violinist in the Vienna Philharmonic Orchestra.

The mild reception which Fritz received as a violinist convinced his father that the boy's future lay in directions other than music. And so the violin was put aside —permanently, it was then believed. Fritz was enrolled in the Vienna Gymnasium to prepare for the career of medicine. For several years he conformed to the strict discipline of student life, and revealed an astonishing adaptability for his studies. Then, somewhat impatient with the routine, he suddenly decided to reassume an artistic life. The violin he still avoided scrupulously. This time he felt the call for painting, and not for music. He left for Paris, worked hard there and received the glowing praises of Julien. He then came to Rome for further intensive study. Finally, the lure of art having palled just as he was about to achieve success with it, Fritz returned to Vienna to prepare for a stiff army examination. He passed with high honors. For a full year he wore the uniform of an officer in the regiment at the Uhlans.

Soldiering, however, could never appeal permanently to a person of Kreisler's keen intellect. So he abandoned it—once again with success awaiting him in his newly chosen profession. Since no other career was open to him, he returned—not a little reluctantly, he confesses—to the violin.

His former suppleness of fingers was gone, so Kreisler decided to retire to the country for eight weeks of indefatigable practising. He worked assiduously, pouring his entire devotion, energy, and application into his technique. And he emerged from this eight-week period of retirement and study the greatest violinist of his generation.

5

He made his return début in Berlin in 1899, but several years passed before his concerts received something more than a cordial but apathetic response. "I was as great a fiddler then as I have been ever since," Kreisler informs us; but his playing failed to inflame the imagination of his public. Avoiding the shallow and the sensational, placing less emphasis upon pyrotechnics and more upon musical content, Kreisler's performances were too serious for immediate recognition.

However, when his full stature finally became apparent—particularly with his grandiose conception of the Bach solo sonatas for violin, and the violin concertos of Bach, Beethoven and Brahms—it was America that was one of the first countries to give him full recognition. After several tours through this country, from 1901 to 1903, which were nothing short of sensational, his supreme position among the violinists of his day could no longer be subject to question.

While en route to America in 1902, Fritz Kreisler

met aboard ship a charming American woman, Harriet Lies. Their friendship developed rapidly. In November of that year they were married. Theirs was a marriage of true minds, which has offered no little inspiration and strength to the great violinist.

When the War broke out in Europe in 1914, Kreisler was vacationing in Switzerland. Without the hesitation of a moment—Viennese blood is hot blood!—he returned to his country to rejoin his former troops which had been stationed in Galicia. All the gruesome privations of a soldier's life were now the fate of the world's greatest violinist. "For two days I went without taking off my clothes," Kreisler himself wrote in reminiscing of his weeks in the trenches,[1] "sleeping on wet grass, or in the mud, or in the swamps. One night, while sleeping, we were drenched to the skin by torrential rains. . . . We were looking like shaggy wolves from the necessity of subsisting on next to nothing. I remember having gone for more than three days at a time without any food whatsoever, and many a time we had to lick the dew from the grass for want of water."

On September 6, 1914, an unexpected cavalry attack from the Russians descended upon Lemberg, and Kreisler was a victim. A lance pierced his foot. With the help

[1] *Four Weeks in the Trenches,* by Fritz Kreisler. Houghton Mifflin Company, 1915.

Arturo Toscanini

of an orderly he made his way safely to the hospital.

Discharged from the army with high honors, Kreisler felt that there was only one avenue left through which he could help his country. He undertook an extensive concert tour through America which would have sapped the energy and exhausted the strength of a physique stronger than his. But he could do this bravely and cheerfully because he knew that his bulging income would bring relief to his crushed compatriots.

With America's entry into the War, Kreisler's position in this country became embarrassing. He had been a soldier in the enemy's camp. He had openly confessed that his earnings from concerts were sent to Austria to relieve suffering. He was too honest to renounce his allegiance to the country of his birth simply because the expedience of the moment demanded it. He therefore found abuse and antagonism, insult and hate descending upon him from pulpit and press, from ladies' forums and patriotic societies. Only one move remained for Kreisler: He announced his retirement from concert work and escaped to Maine where, in a deserted corner, he could find consolation in his violin, in gardening, and in the playing of chess.

In the winter of 1919, Fritz Kreisler once again emerged from retirement to appear on the concert platform. The concert in which he first made his reappearance will never be forgotten by those of us who were present. When he stepped on the stage of Carnegie Hall in New York, an entire audience—now recovering from its former war hysteria—rose spontaneously to welcome him. For more than five minutes it remained on its feet in honor of a great artist, but a still greater personality.

And it has remained on its feet ever since.

MEN AND WOMEN WHO MAKE MUSIC

II: TOSCANINI

ARTURO TOSCANINI

FOR a brief year and a half, between May of 1936 and December of 1937, Toscanini was absent from the American music scene; and the feeling was strong among many music lovers that a temporary music depression had automatically set in.

Toscanini—whose big stick had directed the New York Philharmonic Symphony Society for ten years, creating a standard of orchestral performance which remained unequaled throughout the world—had said permanent farewell to America in the Spring of 1936. Feeling that the gap left vacant by Toscanini could never be filled by any other conductor, or group of conductors, the National Broadcasting System made herculean efforts the following year to bring the Italian maestro back to America. They started a special orchestra for him which included famous musicians culled from different parts of America and Europe. They provided him with working conditions to satisfy his most fastidious requirements as an artist: a sufficient number of rehearsals, full liberty in the planning of the programs, complete control of the artistic policies of the orchestra, and a promise that the concerts would never be commercialized. They gave him a fabulous salary, and (the medium of radio being what it is) a weekly audience of several million listeners.

Toscanini finally yielded, consenting to conduct ten consecutive weeks of radio concerts. It was costing the National Broadcasting System a quarter of a million dollars to restore Toscanini to American music lovers. Considering Toscanini's position in the world of music, the price was a bargain.

When on Christmas night of 1937, music lovers throughout America tuned in on the first of the Toscanini concerts, they were listening not only to the world's greatest conductor, but also to one who—in his own day —has become something of a legend with the music public. Few musicians of our generation have had the capacity to inflame the imagination of a music world as has Toscanini. The conductor's platform on which he stands becomes instantly bathed with glamour; the concert hall in which he appears becomes alive with electric currents. One has merely to recall the queue which patiently encircled Carnegie Hall for ten hours trying to gain admission to his farewell American concert in 1936, or to bring to mind the brilliant and cosmopolitan audiences that traveled for several summers to the Salzburg music festival in Austria (from points as far remote as Buenos Aires, California and Bombay) to hear him conduct opera, to realize the peculiarly potent magnetism of the man.

Toscanini's hold on the imagination of a world-wide public is not difficult to explain, nor his ability to inspire fabulous stories. He has the material which goes into the making of public idols. His phenomenal musical gifts inevitably inspire wonder and awe: his memory which has absorbed in its sponge-like tissues the entire symphonic repertoire and the bulk of operatic literature; his phenomenal ear which can pierce the most inextricable mazes of orchestral sonority and pluck from it a wrong note or an ill-adjusted nuance; his prodigious ability to make an orchestra play, and singers sing, as no other conductor of recent memory has succeeded in doing.

But it is not his genius alone that has encircled a halo about his head. His personality is such as to excite the imagination of the masses. His reticence and impenetrable aloofness have spread about him an intriguing cloak of mystery. His volatile personality—his volcanic bursts of temper and, at other moments, his almost angelic serenity—inject a dramatic note into everything he says and does. The vibrancy of his personality charges the atmosphere in which he appears, acting almost hypnotically on both the audience and the musicians who perform under his baton.

Added to these personal attributes of Toscanini there are his unsurpassable humility and modesty, his unblemished integrity as an artist, his complete preoccupation with his art. Music to him is a religious ritual in which he is a high priest. Thus he completely disregards—even flees from—those things for which so many other artists struggle: personal glorification, applause and adulation, pomp and ceremony.

There is, finally, a rich vein of nobility in him which sets him apart from so many other musicians. The same fierce honesty and high idealism which he has brought to music he likewise brings to living. Expediency and diplomacy do not exist for him; only truth and virtue. He has fearlessly expressed his antagonism toward Fascism in his native Italy, and has even suffered personal abuse rather than perform the Fascist hymn at one of his concerts. When his native Italy embarked on its anti-Semitic program he was not afraid to voice his open contempt of such a policy, even though he was in Italy at the time and open to retaliatory attacks by the government which, truth to tell, were not slow in coming. Likewise, he was one of the first musicians to express open indignation and contempt at the treatment his fellow-artists received

in Germany when the Nazis came into power in 1933.
And when the annexation of Austria by Germany became
a reality, he did not hesitate to express his resentment by
resigning officially from all participation in the Salzburg
festival—even though participation in that festival had
been one of his major interests.

He has never failed to support an important cause, to
rally to an important issue. He—who drives such a hard
financial bargain with those who can afford to pay
his price—has time and again offered his services for
nothing. To mention only two of many instances: Some
twenty years ago he was asked to participate in a monumental festival held to honor the memory of Giuseppe
Verdi, and was asked what his price would be for conducting some of the performances. He refused to accept
even one lira, feeling it sacrilege on his part to be paid
for honoring the memory of a composer whom he had
known personally and whose music he adored. More
recently, he has conducted the Palestine Symphony Orchestra, which consists of exiled German musicians, in
a rigorous traveling schedule which sapped his strength.
Yet, not only did he refuse any remuneration for his
work, but he also declined the offer of traveling expenses.

Qualities such as these are the stuff of which legends
are made.

2

The curious thing about Toscanini is the fact that, although myths have been created about him, the truth is often stranger than the fiction. I have heard stories about Toscanini which I know have been manufactured out of whole cloth. Yet those incidents that have really taken place are much more incredible than the manufactured articles.

There is the matter of his extraordinary ear, for example. I have heard people relate impossible aural feats accomplished by the great conductor, feats which are absurd and incredible. Nor does the fact that they have been invented improve the dramatic quality of these tales. The truth is much more thrilling. Let one violinist in his orchestra fake a difficult passage, and Toscanini's ear will detect it even though sixty violinists are playing simultaneously. I myself attended a rehearsal of Toscanini in which the orchestra was playing a thunderous climax from a modern work. Toscanini abruptly stopped the orchestra to inform the flautist that his accentuation, in a certain phrase, was inexact.

Stories have likewise been invented about his memory. I could, if I had the space, enumerate offhand a half-dozen which Toscanini himself has said are fabricated. But the true ones are much more dramatic. It is well known that Toscanini began his conductorial career in Rio de Janeiro at the age of nineteen, when he was hurriedly called to substitute for an absent conductor in an opera performance. To the amazement of both audience and musicians, Toscanini conducted the opera of the evening—it was *Aïda*—from memory, even though he had never before conducted a note of music. The feat earned for Toscanini the post of permanent conductor with the opera company. And although Toscanini conducted eighteen different operas during this first apprentice year, not once did he refer to the printed page!

Since that historic début, Toscanini's career has spanned fifty years and has brought him to the four corners of the world. He has directed standard works, unfamiliar and forgotten old music, and new compositions fresh from manuscript, both in the symphony hall and the opera house. In fifty years, his baton has carved the performance of what must surely constitute the bulk of musical literature. Yet in all this time and through all these works, Toscanini has directed from memory. I am certain that musical history would be at a loss to duplicate such a feat.

That man remembers every note, and every marking on the printed page of every score he conducts. One time a double-bassoon player came to him before a rehearsal and told Toscanini that something had gone wrong with his instrument which made it impossible for him to sound the note of E-flat. Toscanini buried his head in his hands, spent several moments in intense concentration, and then told the musician: "That's all right. The note of E-flat does not appear in your music today." Toscanini will receive a new composition, never before performed, on a Friday afternoon, and the following Monday he is able to direct the rehearsals from memory. Upon one occasion when he accomplished this feat he even went so far as to correct the composer himself, who happened to be present, in certain nuances which had been definitely marked in the manuscript but which the composer (who was playing the piano part) had forgotten.

The Toscanini legend, as it is repeated from mouth to mouth, lays particular emphasis upon his capricious temperament. Stories of his Italian temper, his mercilessly rigid disciplining of his musicians, his erratic personal idiosyncrasies, his inflexible iron will form the bulk of the anecdotal material about him. Here, I think, legends have far outdistanced the truth, and in many instances do not do justice to the man.

It is quite true that hell hath no fury like Toscanini's when a musical performance or rehearsal does not go well. In Carnegie Hall he once punched in a thin wooden cabinet because a Wagnerian number had not gone smoothly. In his younger days he was not above throwing a music stand at the unsuspecting head of an erring musician, while today he still yields at times to tantrums of rage and violence at mistakes. Not so long ago at a rehearsal—which went badly—his rage became uncontrollably explosive. He hurled his music stand to the floor and broke his baton into bits. Whipping his handkerchief from the back pocket he tried to tear it but, made of strong fiber, it refused to yield. Toscanini then threw the handkerchief aside impatiently, removed his alpaca jacket and proceeded to tear that to shreds.

Yet Toscanini's temper, I know, has been greatly exaggerated. He can be the most sweet-tempered and docile of men. He demands, of course, the most exacting discipline from his performers, is importunate in his demand for perfection of performance. But he is far from being unreasonable. He can rehearse a passage of music twenty times in succession without losing his equanimity. Usually, he explains his desires quietly and simply, and if his explanation has not been comprehended, he will repeat his demands a second or a third time. It is only after prolonged rehearsal, when he finally feels incapable of transmitting his conception of a work to his musicians, that he yields first to despair and then to frenzy. At such moments his temper is cataclysmic. He explodes the hot lava of invective upon his musicians. He weeps with humiliation. Then he will go off in a corner, sulk in his seat, bury his head in his hands and sigh and moan to himself. The musicians know, however, that these storms are brief, and wait quietly for them to subside. When they do—usually in a few minutes—Toscanini returns to his stand and quietly begins all over again explaining his wishes to the men.

Those who know Toscanini well—particularly the musicians who play under him—realize that his bursts of temper, when they emerge, are not the expression of a pampered and spoiled prima donna, but the outbursts of a profound artist who must always attain perfection in his performances. When a concert goes well, there is no excess temper on the part of Toscanini. Physical discomforts, hard work, petty disturbances cannot cause a ripple on the placid surface of his satisfaction. His face beams sunshine, he giggles, even attempts a far-fetched jest, and is in perfect harmony with the world about him. When performances do not go well, he explodes because he is actually suffering intense physical pain. In New York he used to shut himself in his hotel room for a day, refusing to see anyone, not even touching food. In Salzburg, he was often seen walking with a hasty pace through the streets, an expression of intense pain contracting the muscles of his face.

He is, it is true, a martinet, a man of iron. He dominates his players with dictatorial firmness, demanding from them their last ounce of concentration and attention. His will is as unbending as iron. Yet this man of iron can be soft. Off the platform he adopts toward his musicians a solicitude and affection which are touching. As a matter of fact, those who know Toscanini intimately know only too well that there is a broad streak of sentimentality in him. He is intensely affectionate and warm, sometimes melting with his feelings. He has been known to weep like a schoolgirl upon hearing beautiful music. Characteristic of the softness of his make-up was the dramatic first performance of Puccini's *Turandot*. The composer, who was a dear friend of Toscanini, died while the composer was still in the process of composition, and at Toscanini's wish the work was performed under his baton in its uncompleted state. At the performance of the opera, therefore, the work came to a sudden halt, the music stopping in the very middle of a phrase. Toscanini put down his baton, turned around to the audience and—with tears pouring down his face—called out: "Here—here—the master died!"

Not prima donna temperament but a profound artistic conscience makes him flee from the applause and adulation of an audience. Throughout his entire career, Toscanini has detested taking bows at the end of a concert or opera, feeling strongly that the audience was deflecting its enthusiasm from the composer to him. He has the

33

supreme modesty of all great men. I am reminded of a rehearsal which I shall never forget, and which I believe I was the first to publicize in print. Toscanini had been rehearsing Beethoven's *Ninth Symphony* with the New York Philharmonic Symphony Society. The orchestra—which had played the work frequently before this—suddenly felt that it was receiving an altogether new insight into the masterpiece, that Toscanini through his penetrating analysis, his magnetic personality and his profound conception had succeeded in laying bare for them the very soul of the music. At the end of the rehearsal, the orchestra could contain itself no longer. The men rose to their feet and cheered the embarrassed little Italian at the top of their voices. For several minutes, Toscanini attempted to arrest their cheering, by waving wildly at them. Finally, when the spontaneous ovation had subsided, Toscanini exclaimed with broken voice—and there were tears glistening in his eyes as he spoke: "You see, gentlemen, it isn't me. . . . It's Beethoven!"

3

What it is that makes Toscanini the greatest conductor in the world; what it is that makes another great conductor like Otto Klemperer exclaim that "a conductor like Toscanini comes only once in a thousand years," can

Ignace Paderewski

be explained almost as easily as the reasons for his magnetic appeal as a personality.

I have already pointed out a part of Toscanini's extraordinary equipment as a conductor: namely, his memory, which makes it possible for him to know every marking of the score and to give it the attention it deserves; his ear, which detects the slightest deviation in performance from what the composer has put on paper; and the vibrancy of his personality, which electrifies the musicians, drawing from them a response which few others could urge.

But this is only a part of Toscanini's powers. Equally important is his uncanny ability to divine the hidden mystery of every score he conducts. His enormous erudition and musical scholarship combine with an infallible taste and instinct in feeling precisely what the composer tried to put on paper. Even early in his career, Toscanini had the capacity to divine the hidden meaning of a composer to a marked degree. During his first years as a conductor in Italy, he directed a performance of Verdi's *Te Deum,* and in one of the passages he instinctively inserted a slow and subtle retard. After the performance, Verdi came to him breathless, embraced him, and exclaimed, "How could you possibly know how to play that passage that way? It is exactly what I had in mind when I wrote it. I did not put that retard in the score because I was afraid that too many conductors would draw it out too long and kill the entire effect." Puccini, the great composer of *Tosca, La Bohème* and *Madame Butterfly*, used to say that "Toscanini conducts a work not just as the written score directs, but as the composer had imagined it in his head even though he failed to write it down on paper." Once, after having directed a Puccini opera, Toscanini was told by the composer, "You have composed this opera a second time."

Toscanini possesses one quality which, unfortunately, is rare among other conductors, a quality which I do not think has ever been sufficiently stressed. He has a phenomenal capacity to retain his freshness for a musical work even though he has directed it a hundred times. He approaches a work like Beethoven's *Fifth Symphony* with the same enthusiasm, humility and attention to detail that he would to a newly discovered masterpiece. Staleness and stagnancy are altogether impossible with him. He has, moreover, a capacity for work which is almost incredible for a man of his years. Driven by his relentless artistic conscience, he can put in eight consecutive hours of indefatigable rehearsing. He is ruthless in his pursuit of perfection; in seeking it, he forgets time, himself and his physical exhaustion. There is no phrase in a musical work that is so negligible as not to receive

36

Toscanini's minute attention. Toscanini himself has frequently said that in rehearsing a musical work, the important passages can frequently take care of themselves; but it is the supposedly unimportant phrase or line that demands careful consideration.

In rehearsal, Toscanini carves each line of music like a sculptor, paying minute attention to every detail of the outline until, finally, he has moulded the entire composition into a work of art. Every means in his power is employed by him to convey his conception of the music to his men. Frequently analysis is not enough. At such times, Toscanini mimes, burlesques, acts. He will fall on his knees, clench his hands in prayer, and cry out to his men: "Gentlemen, please, *pianissimo!*" To suggest a burlesque passage, he will clench his fists, blow up his cheeks, and kick his right foot ("like this the music should sound!"). A subject in one of the Beethoven symphonies, he told his men, should have the movement of a "mother rocking her baby to sleep," while to suggest to his orchestra men the diaphonous quality he was seeking in another Beethoven theme, he whipped his handkerchief from his pocket and dropped it gently in front of him ("the music should fall from the orchestra like a handkerchief"). He bellows and fumes and rages. He pleads and weeps. He groans and snorts. But when his day of work is over, an orchestra has divined the hidden meaning of a musical masterpiece and succeeded in giving it expression.

4

Despite his open hostility to Fascism—and its resentment of his opinions—Toscanini is too much of Italian fiber to separate himself from his native country. He maintains two homes in Italy, one in the city of Milan, and another nearby on one of the beautiful Borromean islands near Stresa. It is at his villa near Stresa that he and his family spend the greater part of the year. There Toscanini—surrounded by the manuscripts and musical mementos of historic importance which grateful musicians and patrons have bestowed upon him, and which he loves to finger—leads a simple life. Occasionally there is music-making, but not frequently. More often other interests occupy the maestro: conversation and long walks with friends who come to visit him; reading—Toscanini is a passionate admirer of Goethe and Dante, Shelley and Shakespeare—; contemplating his collection of paintings. But his favorite pastime is to go through his valuable musical collection, the manuscript letters of Mozart and Verdi, manuscript scores and other items hallowed by the personal touch of the great masters of music. Before these mementos, Toscanini is like a priest in the presence of holiness.

The family circle is a small one. Toscanini's wife, the former ballerina Carla dei Martini, whom he married in 1897—and who renounced her own career to devote herself entirely to her husband—is a remarkable woman. She understands her husband's moods and tempers with an instinct that is sublime, caters to them, and is responsible to a great degree for his peace of mind whenever she is with him. Their daughter, Wanda, and her husband—the great Russian-Jewish pianist Vladimir Horowitz—are frequent visitors at the Toscanini villa; for Wanda is Toscanini's favorite child. Occasionally the other Toscanini children complete the family ring—Walter, Toscanini's only son, and Wally, today the Countess Castelbarco.

Perhaps there on the Borromean island of San Giovanni—in one of the most beautiful settings of all Europe —Toscanini sometimes permits himself the luxury of looking back upon his career as a musician. If he does, he must know the ultimate satisfaction that comes with the realization that his great success had never been bought with impure coin; that always has he been true to his art.

Truly his career has been marked out by the milestones of magnificent achievements. He was born in Parma on March 25, 1867, and as a music student at the Parma Conservatory he frequently arrested the attention of his teachers by playing his lessons from memory. At one time when questioned about his memory, he sat down and wrote down the full orchestral score of the *Lohengrin* prelude.

After he completed his studies at the Conservatory (where he received a diploma with highest honors) he joined the violoncello section of several orchestras. Once again his ability to play his music without consulting the printed page aroused considerable admiration among musicians. He next joined the orchestra of an itinerant opera company which was scheduled for a tour of South America. It was during this tour—the year was 1886—that he made his dramatic début as a conductor.

Returning to Italy, he directed opera in Turin, and the notices he received from the critics approached the adulatory. He conducted opera in the leading cities of Italy until 1898, when—now recognized as one of the greatest living Italian conductors—he was appointed permanent conductor of the world famous La Scala opera house in Milan. Only thirty-one years old, and permanent conductor at one of the great opera houses of the world!

What he accomplished in the ten year period between

1898 and 1909 in bringing La Scala to a position of unparalleled importance among the opera houses of Europe is now musical history. He shattered the insularity of the Italians by introducing to them the great German, Russian and French works never before performed in Italy. The repertoire of La Scala was revitalized and expanded; the performances of German operas by Weber, Wagner, Gluck—whipped into shape by the indefatigable and merciless demands of the new director —achieved a standard thought impossible for an Italian opera company.

Then, his fastidious and relentless demands for perfection—which insisted upon more rehearsals than they would give him—brought about a rupture between Toscanini and La Scala. In 1908 he came to America to direct opera at the Metropolitan Opera House for seven years. The story of his magnificent régime at the Metropolitan is too well known to bear repetition here. Unfortunately, in 1915, a serious altercation between him and Gatti-Casazza (which has never been adequately explained but which may have arisen from Toscanini's demands for additional rehearsals and his insistence on bending the will of the singers to his demands) took Toscanini back to Italy.

From 1920 to 1929, Toscanini was the musical director of his old opera house, La Scala. These were years of opera making which music lovers in Italy, and pilgrims from the rest of Europe, will probably never forget. Then, from 1926 until 1936, Toscanini brought ten magnificent years of symphony performances to the New York Philharmonic Symphony Society, making this orchestra unequaled among the musical institutions of the world. In 1930 he was the first foreign conductor invited to direct Wagner's operas at Bayreuth, and the miracles he achieved with *Tannhäuser, Tristan* and *Parsifal,* caused more than one German pundit to disbelieve his ears in amazement. After 1934 he made the Salzburg festival the greatest music center in Europe, with his performances of operas by Wagner, Verdi, Mozart and Beethoven; as long as he remained in Salzburg, so long did it remain the musical Mecca of the world.

Today, his seventieth birthday already behind him, he is still carving musical history. He is fulfilling a three-year contract with the National Broadcasting Company, spreading his art through the medium of radio to the largest music audience the world has known.

That man does not need legends to glorify him. He is a legend unto himself.

III: PADEREWSKI

CHAPTER THREE

IGNACE JAN PADEREWSKI

PADEREWSKI'S day as a pianist is virtually ended. But his name has lost none of its lustre. His last concert tour in this country took place as recently as Spring of 1939. No doubt he has passed his prime as an artist: his former staggering technique has today less certainty— less consummate is his command of the resources of the piano. But something of the old Paderewski—the Paderewski who electrified the whole musical world—is still present whenever he plays. Whether he performs Haydn, Beethoven, Schumann, Chopin or Liszt, he has still his one-time prodigious capacity to transmute human experience into tones. Some have called him the "poet of the piano"; others, the "philosopher of the keyboard." But either designation—or any other—is futile in adequately describing his capacity to endow the music he plays with implications quite outside the realm of music. Architectural design of a musical work, or the virtuosity of its performance, has never concerned us consciously when Paderewski was at the piano. We did not derive from his playing a sensuous thrill, to roll at the tip of our tongue deliciously before digesting it. With Paderewski, music became a titanic emotional experience which left the listener limp with exhaustion.

The poetic fire which set aflame his Beethoven, Chopin, Schumann, is a quality which time can never destroy. Nor could time affect his personality, which galvanised an audience by its very presence, or his profound musical erudition, or his all-embracing culture or his taste, or his limitless imagination. Thus Paderewski —whatever his technical shortcomings may now be—is still among the immortals of the keyboard, just as he was almost a half century ago. Then he ranked with Rubinstein, Busoni and Liszt; today he stands with Hofmann, Schnabel and Gieseking. Surely of no other musician can it be said with such justification: "His story is the story of modern piano-playing."

2

He has made two worlds his—that of music and that of politics. Sometimes the two worlds became one when, with his beloved Chopin, he was able to give musical expression to his profound Polish nationalism. At such moments, Paderewski—who has played so many things magnificently—was truly the incomparable artist.

He was early made conscious of both music and Polish

nationalism, and they have dominated his life ever since. He was three years old when he first became aware of the Polish problem. Ignace Jan Paderewski was born on November 6, 1860 in Podolia, then under Russian rule, but one time a province of the old Polish republic. His family was composed of Polish patriots who dreamed of freeing Poland from foreign subjugation. His mother, who was the daughter of a university professor banished from Poland to Siberia, had been born in exile; his father was active in secret nationalistic movements.

In his third year, Ignace saw the Cossacks descend upon his home, ransack the place, and arrest his father. That scene left an indelible impression upon him. It became the root of his later fiery nationalistic ardor.

Music also became a part of his life when he was still very young. His mother, who died during his infancy, had been an accomplished pianist. Music was an important part of the Paderewski household. And to music, Ignace showed first signs of response shortly after his third birthday.

After about a year in prison, Paderewski's father was released. He changed his home to Volhynia where he found employment as administrator of a vast estate.

Soon music became a dominating force in the boy's life. At the age of six he began the study of the piano— curiously, under a violinist. The instruction was bad, and

Ignace learned little. One year later, he became a pupil of Pierre Sowinski, from whom he received his first intensive systematic training. From that moment on, he made swift strides. He was a remarkable pupil, quick to learn his lessons, and painfully conscientious. Hours were spent by him in practice at the piano. For diversion he often turned to the composition of small pieces for the piano.

He soon discovered Chopin. Chopin became for him much more than the romantic yearnings of a tone-poet who sang nocturnes and ballades so beautifully. Chopin became for him the voice of his enslaved Poland. He became for him the expression of many things which were integral parts of the Paderewski household but which were suppressed and smothered. "All was forbidden us —the language and faith of our fathers, our national dress, our songs, our poets," Paderewski later said. "Chopin alone was not forbidden us. . . . In him we could still find the living breath of all that was prohibited. . . . He gave all back to us, mingled with the prayers of broken hearts, the revolt of fettered soul, the pain of slavery, lost Freedom's ache, the cursing of tyrants, the exultant songs of victory."

The above quotation is, perhaps, the most eloquent explanation of why Paderewski, in the prime of his career, was the incomparable interpreter of Chopin. He found in Chopin so much more than other pianists have. Chopin set his poetic soul aflame. Through Chopin he spoke his own life's struggles, dreams, ideals. The polonaises and mazurkas were much more than great music to him; they were a part of his life's blood.

Despite his great preoccupation with music, he was a normal and healthy boy, very sociable and well liked. He was fond of outdoor sports, climbed trees with as much gusto as his friends, went swimming and horse back riding frequently. Childish games were dear to him, and he recalls that as a boy he enjoyed nothing quite so much as playing soldier with his friends.

He was twelve years old when he gave his first concert, together with his sister. After that he made two or three appearances by himself. These concerts were powerful indications of his extraordinary gifts. His teacher, Sowinski, finally prevailed upon Paderewski's father to permit the boy to go to Warsaw and enter the Conservatory.

In Warsaw, Paderewski knew "years and years of toil, pain and study." They were important years of growth and development. For four years, he worked hard with that enormous concentration and application of which he had always been, and always was to be, capable. At the end of the first year he won first prize for composition and piano. He was subjected to innumerable important musical influences. He met personally such great musicians as Rubinstein, von Bülow, Joachim, Wieniawski, heard them play, and was strongly influenced by their art. He attended the opera religiously, fell under the spell of such native Polish operas as *Halka* and the Italian repertory.

His school career, however, did not run altogether smoothly. He was hot-headed, fiercely independent, intransigent when he felt that the rules of the Conservatory were an infringement on his personal liberty. Twice he was expelled. But, fortunately, there were always satisfactory adjustments between the rebellious student and his stringent masters. He worked hard at the piano and at composition, and was the pride of his teachers. Six years after he entered the Conservatory, he graduated with high honors.

Immediately after graduation, he was appointed instructor of the intermediate piano classes at the Conservatory. The income was shabby, less than twenty-five cents an hour. But to Paderewski it meant the fulfillment of a dream. In his senior year he had fallen in love with a classmate, Antonina Korsak. He was now in a position to marry her.

That first year of marriage was idyllic. Paderewski did not mind the hard work at the Conservatory, or the long hours of night which he spent in study and composition. He had found happiness in the home. More than that, he had found some recognition as a composer, for his first published piano piece, an *Impromptu in F-major*, had just made its appearance.

And then, suddenly, tragedy. His wife died in child-birth, one of the greatest personal blows that Paderewski was to experience.

He could stay in Warsaw no longer. He decided to go to Berlin for more study and development. He plunged deliriously into musical activity, made important contact with such great musicians as Richard Strauss, Eugen D'Albert and Pablo de Sarasate, studied composition under Friedrich Kiel and applied himself industriously to the piano. He worked so hard—often twelve hours consecutively—that his nerves gave way. After one year, he was forced to return to Warsaw and reassume his position at the Conservatory.

In Berlin, he had performed his own *Variations in A-minor* for Anton Rubinstein. Rubinstein, who had thought of Paderewski only as a composer, now recognized in him the promise of greatness as a virtuoso. He advised Paderewski to consider seriously becoming a concert artist. Such words from Rubinstein were not to be taken lightly. They haunted Paderewski for a long time. Until now, he had hoped to make his mark as a composer. Now, for the first time, he thought of becoming a virtuoso largely in the hope of eventually obtaining more leisure.

After another visit to Berlin, for more study, he gave a concert of his own works in Warsaw. The praise he received for his playing was so great as to confirm him in his new decision. But his ever-severe conscience, integrity and self-criticism told him forcefully that more study was necessary before he exhibited himself. He was dissatisfied with his technique—it required greater precision, despatch, cleanliness of attack. He was dissatisfied with his repertoire—it was too limited.

He needed now, he felt, intensive study under an acknowledged master. His eyes turned toward Vienna, the home of Theodor Leschetizky.

3

Early in 1884, Paderewski arrived in Vienna, and introduced himself to Leschetizky. Leschetizky was familiar with some of Paderewski's compositions and admired them; but was reluctant to accept him as his pupil. "It is too late, far too late," he cried. "You can't become a great pianist because you wasted your time studying things more pleasant for yourself, such as counterpoint and orchestration."

Finally Leschetizky yielded, but only on the condition that Paderewski obey him implicitly, follow his orders with slavish devotion. He subjected Paderewski to rigid discipline with—of all things!—Czerny exercises and simple Beethoven sonatas. One bar was studied at a time, subjected to a minute and painstaking analysis. One page was the work of a full day. For eight to ten hours, Paderewski practised at his home.

One year later, Paderewski's course of study was temporarily abandoned when he assumed (upon the advice of Leschetizky) the post of professor of the piano at the Conservatory of Strasbourg. But his self-criticism soon brought him back to the Carl Ludwigstrasse, back to Leschetizky, back to his days of severe discipline and study.

In 1887, Leschetizky acknowledged that Paderewski had achieved the miraculous. He had overcome his early unsatisfactory training and had arrived at full command of his technique. In autumn of that year, Leschetizky arranged for Paderewski to appear on a concert program featuring the Italian singer, Pauline Lucca. Paderewski played some Beethoven, some Chopin and his own *Variations*. "I remember well the night that Leschetizky brought out his brilliant pupil, Ignace Jan Paderewski," later wrote the Countess Angela Potocki. "His performance of an original theme and variations was greeted with special favor. . . . Yet, as he stood nonchalantly in the passageway, his tawny head resting against the wall, those who foresaw his great future were probably few."

Few, indeed! One Viennese musician said to Leschetizky after the performance: "This young man does not seem to promise much."

"My dear sir," Leschetizky answered quietly, "you will have to get used to hearing that young man's name."

A few months later, Paderewski gave a concert at the Salle Érard in Paris, featuring the thirty-two variations of Beethoven and the Sixth Hungarian Rhapsody of Liszt. The distinguished audience included Tschaikovsky (who was then visiting Paris), Gounod, Saint-Saëns, and the great French conductors, Colonne and Lamoureux. The concert was a sensation. "He was always a master of himself," one critic wrote. "He phrases admirably, shades with simplicity, keeps measure with rigorous exactness yet never shows stiffness. He obtains a large sonority by attack and enforcement. He knows his effects beforehand, and yet in spite of this assurance he seems to play as if by inspiration." After the performance, Lamoureux and Colonne rushed backstage to beg Paderewski to appear with their orchestras. An excited manager came to engage him for a series of concerts in Paris.

He made a second successful appearance in Paris, and then insisted upon returning to Vienna for further study before undertaking more concerts. The preparation of a program was ever no small task for him. Each composition he played was the result of a dissection so painstaking—phrase by phrase, bar by bar; and even when the conception of a work was carefully thought out, there was so much experiment necessary with the pedals, with the touch and the tone, with the phrasing and dynamics, that his repertoire was inevitably a small one.

Once again he was with Leschetizky, enlarging his repertoire under the critical guidance of his master. Then, early in 1889, he gave a recital at the hall of Bösendorfer, the piano manufacturer. It was to this concert—and not to his successful appearance in Paris—that Paderewski later referred to as his *"real* début." "That concert attracted a very large audience. . . . The critics of Vienna received me with great enthusiasm. Here is perhaps the moment that I may say they hailed me as a 'great star.' My career as a pianist was launched. There was solid ground under my feet at last."

His career as a composer was also fully launched. A few months later, his Piano Concerto in A-minor was introduced by Mme. Essipoff-Leschetizky at the concerts of the Vienna Philharmonic Orchestra, Hans Richter conducting. Its success was immediate.

He was back in Paris in the fall of 1889 to give three concerts in honor of the Exposition. He was the sensation of musical Paris, fêted in the leading salons of the city, the admiration of the foremost musicians, and the subject for conversation among the dilettantes of the cafés.

Warming to Paris as to no other city, not even Vienna which he loved, he decided to make it his home. He rented a small ground floor apartment on the Avenue Victor Hugo, which was to remain his home until 1906. From then on he rubbed elbows with the musical great of Paris and was one of them—Gounod, Saint-Saëns, Massenet, Widor, Fauré and Vincent D'Indy.

Having conquered Vienna and Paris, he was eager for further triumphs. In 1890, he went to England and made his début at St. James' Hall. The weather was bad on the day of his concert; Paderewski was unusually nervous. The concert was a failure. One critic said of Paderewski that he made "much noise, but no music." In his next three appearances, however, he redeemed himself. The fourth concert, devoted entirely to Chopin, was sold out—and was rapturously praised. There followed an enormously successful tour in the provinces. Paderewski now became as celebrated in England as in France and Austria.

His next, and perhaps greatest, victory came in America. In 1891 he crossed the ocean and on November 17 made his first appearance at Carnegie Hall, performing his own Concerto in A-minor and the Saint Saëns

C-minor Concerto. "He is one of those virtuosi to whom the keyboard has no hidden secrets," wrote James Gibbons Huneker. "His technical equipment is perfect and is used in such an exquisitely musical fashion that the virtuoso merges ever into the artist and mere brutal display and brilliant charlatanry are totally absent. . . . There is life about his work, a transfiguration of some simple musical idea, that is inspiration in itself. His ability hinges perilously on the gates of genius. He is a veritable artistic apparition, and with that supremely magnetic personality, graceful and exotic in appearance, he naturally scored a success that was stupendous."

So stupendous that, when he had given three concerts with orchestra at Carnegie Hall, he was compelled to given an additional series at Madison Square Garden.

In later years, recalling these concerts of Paderewski in New York, James Gibbons Huneker wrote: "His tone was noble, his technic adequate, his single-finger touch singing. Above all, there was a romantic temperament exposed; not morbid but robust. . . . Many have gone to gaze upon him, but they remained to listen. His solid attainments as a musician, his clear, elevated style, his voluptuous, caressing touch, his sometimes exaggerated sentiment, his brilliancy, endurance and dreamy poetry —these qualities are real, not imaginary. . . . No more luscious touch has been heard since Rubinstein's. . . .

No one since Rubinstein—in America at least—can create such climaxes of enthusiasm. . . . There is the feeling, when you hear him, that he is a complete man, a harmonious artist, and this feeling is very compelling." [1]

From New York, Paderewski embarked on an extensive tour of the country—a tour which was destined to be the first of many he was to pursue in the next forty years. His triumph followed him everywhere like an attending maid.

Then came performances in Russia, Australia, New Zealand, Germany.

By the turn of the new century, he was considered by many one of the greatest musical figures of the generation.

4

Indisputable his genius as a recreator of piano literature! Yet Paderewski's enormous triumph throughout the world would have been less instantaneous, and less impressive, were not his personality as magnetizing as his performances. He cut an unforgettably picturesque figure at the piano. His large head appeared poetic, throbbing with the music. It was a head which, as Helena Modjeska wrote, "looked like one of Botticelli's or Fra Angelico's angels" with "its aureole of profuse golden

[1] *Franz Liszt*, by James Gibbons Huneker. New York, 1911.

hair and almost feminine features." It was a head, spiritual and almost other-worldly—qualities which Burne-Jones caught so magically in his famous portrait.

At the piano, he commanded attention through the sheer strength of his personality. The audience could feel the presence of a dominating force, could almost feel his herculean strength and fanatical will as he walked to the piano and sat down in front of the keyboard. The dynamic energy which seemed to be pent up within him discharged an electric current throughout the concert hall when Paderewski was at the piano. The audience sat electrified—even before he put his hands on the keys.

On the stage, the cloak of glamour which enveloped him seemed to set him apart from the everyday world. Yet, as his friends have known, he could be, off the platform, human, sympathetic and very much of the world. He is not beyond human frailities—finding pleasure in playing cards and sometimes indulging in all-night bridge sessions; confessing that nothing offers him such complete relaxation as a good motion picture. He plays billiards frequently, and is quite expert at it. He smokes prodigiously—yet he is no slave to the cigarette. Once he gave up smoking for a year merely to convince himself that he was a complete master over his habits. Then, when he had convinced himself of it, he returned to smoking.

He has had an almost hypochondriac absorption in his health. He has always been passionately devoted to gymnastics, and has watched his diet and physique as carefully as a pugilist might. This has, however, not been wasted. Even today he is well-built and muscular. His strong body has well withstood the strain and stress of an active musical and political career.

Few will doubt that Paderewski is today the most decorated musician alive. Commander of the Crown of Italy, Commander of the Order of Carlos Tercero of Spain, Grand Officer of the Legion of Honor of France, Grand Cross of the Polish Orders of Polonia Restituta and of the White Eagle, Knight Commander of the British Empire—these are only a few of the many distinctions he has received. More recently, Italy bestowed upon him the rank of the Grand Cross of the Order of St. Lazare and Maurice, and the Swiss government has given him honorary citizenship.

During his more recent tours of this country, Paderewski has traveled by private deluxe train. This train boasts of the comforts of home—and contains a piano, Paderewski's favorite books, comfortable chairs, a private lighting and heating system so that it can be sidetracked without losing any comforts, and sometimes even three additional bridge players. It is connected by telephone with every city where Paderewski must stop for a concert. Its entourage of eight people includes a chef to prepare Paderewski's rigorously watched diet.

5

Having conquered the world of music with his art, Paderewski, suddenly—in 1905—was attacked by a neurotic condition which brought about in him a revulsion for the piano. He felt that he was no longer able to transmute his thoughts through the keyboard. More than that, playing brought him actual physical pain. He consulted one physician after another. One of them advised him to retire from concert work and to devote himself to farming. Paderewski bought some land, cows, pigs and other live-stock and, deserting the piano completely, became an active farmer.

Unfortunately his adventures in farming proved so costly that they absorbed all his funds. There was no alternative left for him but to return to the concert stage. He played in Switzerland, then toured America. It was a trying experience. His detestation of the piano had not left him, and he continued to play only through the herculean strength of his will. But his tour in America came to an abrupt end. His neurotic ailment had brought about a slight paralysis of the fingers.

Once again he abandoned the piano. For the first time

he turned his energy into politics. He raised funds for the erection of a monument in Warsaw to commemorate the battle of Grünwald. At its unveiling he made a short speech—probably his first excursion into politics. That same year, he made another speech, this time in honor of Chopin. At both occasions he was given a tremendous reception by his countrypeople, which proved to him that his appeal before a public did not rest entirely with the piano.

But he was in pressing financial difficulties. His fingers having recovered slightly, he decided to attempt another concert tour. He played in South America, then in South Africa, and finally in the United States. Though each concert was to him physical torture, he continued his tour bravely. But always in the back of his mind was the hope that he could soon give up the playing of the piano permanently.

They were celebrating Paderewski's name-day at his home in Switzerland, on the evening of July 31, 1914, when news arrived by telephone that Europe was on the brink of war. When war broke out, Paderewski turned his magnificent energy into helping his country. He gave concerts, the funds from which were directed toward succoring Polish victims. He personally organized committees in Paris and London to aid the Polish. In 1915, he came to America not only to raise funds for Poland,

62

but even more to arouse American interest in the Polish problem. For five years, he played and he spoke—and did both eloquently. "I have to speak about a country which is not yours, in a language which is not mine," he told his hearers with touching simplicity. But his message fell on fertile soil. It was largely through his efforts that the freedom of Poland became the thirteenth of President Wilson's Fourteen Points.

In 1919, Paderewski, heading the national party, was elected the first president of a united, independent and autonomous Poland.

He had seen the realization of a life-long dream in the emergence of a free Poland. As its first leader, he had carried it through its first precarious year of existence. Then, in 1920, he abandoned politics, returned to America—and to his first love, music. Although he had already passed his sixtieth birthday, he was thinking of another world tour as a concert pianist. For several years, he returned to the study of the piano, with the diligence and assiduity of a young artist about to embark on a career. He restudied his repertoire with an attention to detail as if he were approaching the music for the first time. Then, in 1922, he announced that he was ready for concert appearances.

Fortunately, there was nothing anti-climactic in his return to the concert platform. His technique was, perhaps, less assured, but the sublimity of his musical conceptions remained unblemished. Once again, as at the turn of the century, his march through the world of music was on a path of glory.

His public had not forgotten him.

IV: FLAGSTAD

Kirsten Flagstad
in Lohengrin

CHAPTER FOUR

KIRSTEN FLAGSTAD

THEY have been saying that there has recently taken place in New York a rebirth of enthusiasm for the music dramas of Richard Wagner. Since 1935, Wagner has been performed at the Metropolitan Opera House almost three times as frequently as any other composer, and almost always to sold-out houses. *Tristan und Isolde* alone grossed $150,000 in nine performances, making it the biggest single hit that Broadway has known.

Yet to say that New York opera lovers have suddenly rediscovered Wagner would be to state only half a truth. It would be more accurate to say that New York opera lovers rediscovered Wagner through the interpretative genius of a new singer.

She came here unknown and unheralded. After two performances, she became the greatest consistent box-office attraction that the Metropolitan has had since Caruso. Single-handed, this new amazing artist brought prosperity back to the Metropolitan during some of the leanest financial years in its history. Even more formidable a feat, she silenced forever those gray-beards who

67

for years have been boring us with their reminiscences of Emmy Destinn, Fremstad and Nordica. There was no longer a need for talking about the long-lost golden age of Wagnerian opera. The golden age of Wagnerian opera was here again.

When captious remarks are made about the musical intelligence of opera audiences or about the discernment of music critics, it might be wise to recall the evening of February 2, 1935 at the Metropolitan Opera House. A new soprano, Kirsten Flagstad, had come from Scandinavia to make her début as Sieglinde in Wagner's *Die Walküre*. The number in that audience who had heard the name of Kirsten Flagstad before this were few and far between. Flagstad had come to this country with no glamorous legends preceding her, nor a triumphant European reputation trailing her. The New York music critic, Oscar Thompson, heard her sing in Oslo in 1932 and spoke well of her, but his review had not attracted much serious attention. None in the audience at the Metropolitan that night could, therefore, suspect that she was above the usual run of perfunctory Wagnerian sopranos. Wagnerian sopranos generally do not emerge with one performance from oblivion to greatness.

Yet she had not been on the stage more than a few minutes when the atmosphere in the opera house became electrified. One could feel the tenseness in the air as though it were some physical substance. At the close of the first act, the audience rose to acclaim the new singer with a spontaneous outburst of enthusiasm, the sincerity of which could not be questioned. The presence of a great singer had been immediately recognized, even though she had come here unpublicized and unknown.

And the next morning. . . . "Mme. Flagstad is that *rara avis* in the Wagnerian woods—a singer with a voice, with looks, with youth," wrote Lawrence Gilman in the *Herald Tribune*. "The voice itself is both lovely and puissant. In its deep register it is movingly warm and rich and expressive, and yesterday it recalled to wistful Wagnerites the irrecoverable magic of Olive the Immortal. The upper voice is powerful and true and does not harden under stress. The singing that we heard yesterday is that of a musician with taste and brains and sensibility, with poetic and dramatic insight. . . . Yesterday was one of those rare occasions when the exigent Richard might have witnessed with happiness an embodiment of his Sieglinde. For this was a beautiful and illusive recreation, poignant and sensitive throughout, and crowned in its greater moments with an authentic exaltation."

Three days after her unforgettable début, the new singer appeared in *Tristan und Isolde*. For the first time in more than twenty-five years, Isolde emerged on the stage a glowing and vibrant figure, a human being swept

69

by forces she herself could not understand, helplessly and inevitably succumbing to a passion which sucked her in like a vortex. Her voice—a supple and incomparably rich instrument—poured from her with facility and opulence.

An Isolde such as this had not been seen or heard on an opera stage since the golden days of Olive Fremstad. No wonder, then, that the audience that night felt that it had just rediscovered Wagner!

2

But for a fortuitous set of circumstances, Kirsten Flagstad might have never made her historic début in New York, and would have retired from opera before her art had achieved full enrichment.

Otto H. Kahn, on a visit to Oslo, heard her in *Tosca* in 1929 (not in 1927, as some reference books have it). He was so impressed by her voice that he urged the Metropolitan Opera House to give her an audition. The Metropolitan immediately wrote to Flagstad asking for the details of her career. To Flagstad this inquiry appeared to be only so much routine on the part of a large opera house, and she did not take it seriously. Moreover, she found the task of translating her Norwegian notices too formidable a job. Finally, she was at the time seriously thinking of renouncing her artistic career for matrimony. She never answered the letter, and her name was momentarily forgotten by the Metropolitan.

In 1934, Eric Simon, the scout from the Metropolitan, heard her sing Sieglinde at Bayreuth and urged Gatti-Casazza and Artur Bodanzky, both then in Switzerland, to give her an audition. Flagstad was only slightly interested in the offer. To appear in the Metropolitan Opera House was, of course, a cherished goal. But she was already married and was more eager than ever to substitute a placid domestic existence for the strenuous life of an opera singer. As a matter of fact, she had already confided to many of her associates that the end of the summer would bring the announcement of her permanent retirement. A few intimate friends, however, urged her to reconsider her decision. Flagstad decided that her audition with the Metropolitan would decide the issue: a contract by the Metropolitan would determine the continuation of her career as a singer; refusal would mean permanent and irrevocable withdrawal from operatic work. Inwardly, she was certain that the Metropolitan would never accept her.

The audition took place in a small hotel room in St. Moritz. On her way to the hotel, Flagstad found a fifty centime piece; that coin—which she has retained as one of her most precious mementos—warned her that good fortune was waiting. She was not nervous, nor uncertain of herself. She sang with full voice, cool and self-assured. But her true stature as an artist was not recognizable at that audition. The small room (which, in addition, was heavily carpeted) disguised the true quality of her singing. Besides Flagstad was asked by Bodanzky to sing the Brünnhilde Immolation music from *Götterdammerung;* and, never having studied the part, she was forced to sing the music at sight. Both Bodanzky and Gatti-Casazza decided that she had a small and limited voice, hardly capable of coping with exacting Wagnerian rôles; but they decided that she sang with insight and intelligence. Then, only because the recent resignation of Frida Leider from the Metropolitan necessitated a hurried replacement, it was decided to give Flagstad a one-season trial in New York.

The officials of the Metropolitan did not even faintly suspect what a strategic *coup* they had made with Flagstad's engagement, or that they had made an epochal discovery. At her first rehearsal at the Metropolitan— it was in *Götterdammerung,* since no rehearsals were scheduled for *Die Walküre,* Flagstad's introductory vehicle—Flagstad's golden voice (which she used, not *mezza voce,* as other singers did in rehearsal, but with full power) flooded the auditorium. Bodanzky put down his baton on the stand and listened, afraid to believe his ears. Paul Althouse was so upset that he missed his cue. It seemed incredible—but there it was! An unknown singer from Scandinavia, who had made only a passable impression at her audition, had a vocal equipment and a stage presence which sent the memories of more than one person at that rehearsal scurrying back more than two decades to find a fitting comparison.

3

When it is recalled that Flagstad's first operatic performance outside of her native Norway did not take place until 1928, that her first Isolde (and her first performance in German) was not sung until 1932, and that her first appearance out of Scandinavia took place as late as 1933, the comparative youth of her artistic career is emphasized fully. However, though Flagstad's career had been short and unsensational before her Metropolitan début, it was not lacking in essential and important vocal experience.

She came from a family of musicians. Her father was an orchestral conductor, and her mother not only conducted opera and operetta but coached so many experienced singers that she was often referred to as "the musical mamma of Norway." A musical heritage was passed on from parents to children. Kirsten, the oldest of the children, made the name of Flagstad world famous. One of her brothers became an orchestral conductor, while another achieved a reputation as a pianist. Her sister, Karen Marie Flagstad Orkel, was for a long time a famous singer of operettas in Vienna.

Born in Oslo on July 12, 1895, Kirsten Flagstad began her musical education at an early age. She was taught the rudiments of the piano, but showed no great aptitude for the instrument. To harmony and counterpoint, or any other theoretical aspect of music, she was sublimely indifferent. Such love for music as she possessed in early childhood was revealed in her singing. At the age of six, she could sing songs of Franz Schubert with a sensitive and refined voice. When she was thirteen, she acquired a complete vocal score of Wagner's *Lohengrin* and was so fascinated by the music that she succeeded in committing to memory the rôle of Elsa.

Flagstad's confirmation was celebrated with a party for friends and relatives, during which she sang arias from *Lohengrin* and *Aïda*. A friend of the family suggested to her that her voice was too fragile for such exacting music, that it might be ruined by abuse. To give her some direction in her singing, the friend offered to give Kirsten a few lessons. This was the first systematic instruction Flagstad received in singing.

She had, however, little hope of becoming a professional singer. She was given an intensive academic education with the hope of preparing her for some career.

Flagstad then studied vocal music seriously for the first time, under Ellen Schytte-Jacobsen in Oslo. For three years she worked on her breathing and tone, practising solfeggio assiduously, and making gradual but important progress. An extended period of study brought greater richness and texture to her voice, so much so that her teacher once told her that two more years of study would enable her to make concert appearances.

A performance of Eugen d'Albert's successful opera, *Tiefland*, was being organized in Oslo. Kirsten Flagstad's mother was at one of the rehearsals during which a candidate for the part of Nuri was being heard and rejected. On her way home, Mme. Flagstad bought a copy of the vocal score and, giving it to her daughter, urged her to study the part. Two days later, Kirsten applied for the rôle. She was the eighteenth candidate, and was accepted.

Flagstad's début as an opera singer took place in her eighteenth year, on December 12, 1913. The impression she made—even though she was cast in a minor rôle—was so good that several important music patrons of Oslo combined to finance her continued study. One year later she made another public appearance as opera singer, this time as Germaine in *The Chimes of Normandy*.

Her study continued first with Albert Westwang and then, for two and a half years, under Gillis Brant in Stockholm. Emerging from this period of retirement and study, she returned to Oslo and made a successful appearance in Wilhelm Kienzl's *Evangelimann*.

In 1919, she was married for the first time—a marriage which ultimately terminated in divorce and concerning which Flagstad prefers to remain secretive. One year later, a girl was born. During this period of pregnancy, Flagstad's voice deserted her; she thought that her career was over. But one day, after her child was born, her mother came to her with music from Lehár's *Zigeuenerliebe*, a performance of which was then being prepared in Oslo. Flagstad sang for her mother—and to the amazement of both, her voice had grown richer, more sensuous and more beautiful.

She was offered, and she accepted, a leading part in the Lehár operetta, and she was a great success. In 1921 Flagstad made an extensive concert tour. Then, returning to Oslo, she became a member of the Mayol Theatre which specialized in the performance of operettas. For two years she appeared in the entire repertoire of great operettas; then, upon leaving the Mayol Theatre, she became a member of the Casino Theatre, to be featured in revues, musical comedies and operettas. But she had not deserted opera. During these years, she also sang in thirty-eight different operas including Gluck's *Orfeo,* Gounod's *Faust* and Bizet's *Carmen.*

Her versatility in singing light and serious music was curiously emphasized one evening in Oslo. She appeared at the Casino Theatre singing a current American "hit" *I Love You! I Love You!* (which she sang half in Norwegian, and half in a curiously accented English). When she finished this performance, she rushed into a taxi and made for the local concert hall where she was scheduled to sing the soprano part in the Oslo Philharmonic performance of Beethoven's *Ninth Symphony.*

In 1928, Flagstad became a member of the Gothenburg Stora Theatre, where she devoted herself entirely to the singing of great operatic music. She soon surpassed all her former triumphs in the field of light music and emphasized, perhaps for the first time, that she was a serious artist of first importance.

Following a performance of *Lohengrin* in 1929, Flagstad was invited to a house-party of Henry Johansen, a wealthy Oslo patron of music, whom she had never before met. Friendship between Flagstad and Johansen developed instantaneously. All night they danced together. The next evening they met for a dinner appointment. The evening after that, they were engaged. Early

77

in 1930, they were married—and from the moment Flagstad became Mrs. Johansen she spoke of withdrawing permanently from her artistic occupation.

For a while, shortly after her marriage, she retired completely from her musical activities, to which she had no intention of ever returning. But after several months, pressure was brought upon her to make a few scattered concert appearances. And the Gothenburg Opera, which had some difficulty with its casting, begged her to return for a few guest performances. In spite of herself, Flagstad drifted back to her career as a singer, then began to accept more and more assignments, and finally acquiesced to the fate which destined her to become the greatest operatic figure of her time.

The milestones in Flagstad's career before her Metropolitan début were not many and can consequently be easily pointed out. Her first German rôles were Elsa and Eva, sung in Norwegian. Isolde, the first rôle which she performed in German, was added to her repertoire in 1932.

Until 1933, her operatic experience was confined to Scandinavia. In that year, she was invited to an audition at Bayreuth. This audition, being successful, resulted in her appearance as Ortlinde and the Third Norn in the Ring drama of Wagner during the festival season of 1933. During her first period in Bayreuth, she continued exercising her voice and developing it, so that at the end of the season Intendant Tiejan of the Bayreuth Festival confessed to her that it was impossible to believe that it was the same voice he had heard at the audition. One summer later, Flagstad sang Sieglinde at Bayreuth.

And then the Metropolitan Opera House.

4

With her first season in New York, Kirsten Flagstad became the cornerstone of the Metropolitan Opera House repertory. During that first season, she sang the rôles of Sieglinde, Isolde, the Brünnhildes of *Walküre* and *Götterdammerung* (both of which she was singing for the first time), and Kundry (also a new rôle for her, committed to memory by her in eighteen days!). When she sang, there were sold-out houses; and she sang frequently. Fortunately, she had been blessed with stamina which has been traditional with great Wagnerian singers. She sang Isolde and Kundry on two successive afternoons; Brünnhilde, Isolde and Eva on three successive evenings—and never showed a visible sign of fatigue. Fortunately, too, she has never pampered her voice but, on the contrary, has always subjected it to rigorous exercise. When she practises, it is always with full voice. Even when she first studied the part of Isolde, which consumes about one hour and a quarter of singing time, she did not restrict the volume of her voice. A long and rigorous season at the Metropolitan, therefore—with several appearances each week—far from bringing any sign of weariness to her singing has, instead, brought it greater depth, intensity and power.

What an all-important place she acquired with the Metropolitan Opera House in her very first season was emphasized the following year. As a gesture of honor to its new star, the Metropolitan, for the first time in thirty-five years, inaugurated a new season with a German opera expressly to feature Flagstad. Queues, long absent from the Metropolitan, encircled the opera house eight hours before curtain time. And at the performance itself, the enthusiasm and outburst of acclaim that honored Flagstad was reminiscent of an age, considered permanently gone, when opera was the life blood of music lovers in New York.

Flagstad's instantaneous sensation in New York is not difficult to explain. On the stage she is an imperial figure, dynamic and magnetizing. Her stage personality is such that it can even inflame the enthusiasm of a public that does not fully comprehend the greatness of her vocal art. I recall that when the motion picture, the *Big Broadcast of 1938,* was first introduced in New York, its featured stars—Martha Raye, Shep Fields, Tito Guizar and W. C. Fields—went through their routines to receive only mild approbation on the part of the audience. But Flagstad, singing the Brünnhilde war-cry from *Die Walküre* (music, the aesthetic implications of which are not easily understandable to a movie public) drew spontaneous outbursts of applause.

Her singing, of course, is a thing of endless glory. She has a great power of voice, an extraordinary compass, and unusual flexibility. Her register is equally rich in both extremes, and she has a luscious *tessitura*. Her tones come freshly and easily, full of roundness and body, each tone attacked cleanly. The greatest dramatic effects in her singing are produced through the simplest of means: with a discreet use of falsetto she can voice a radiant ecstasy; with a carefully selected pause, she can dramatize an entire page of music; a subtle use of variety in her colors, and she can scorch a lyric line with the hot flame of her anger.

In her acting, as in her singing, she is most eloquent when simple. Her gestures are few, but they achieve dramatic effects that are poignant and profound. I recall two decades of Wagnerian sopranos attempting the expression of anguish—with the most elaborate wringing of hands and contortions of body—when, in the last act of *Die Walküre*, Wotan pronounces the expulsion from Valhalla. Yet Flagstad with the simple gesture of turning her head slightly and permitting her eloquently mobile face to grow gray and soft has once and for all given expression to the grief and pain of Brünnhilde. In the same fashion, no hysterical motions of the body are required by Flagstad to speak the ecstasy of a woman in love, in the last scene of *Siegfried*, or the fury of a woman scorned in the second act of *Götterdammerung*—only the contraction or relaxation of her muscles, the softness or hardness of her supple and expressive body.

Flagstad is not, off the stage, an unusually beautiful woman, though her appeal is unquestioned. Yet, like every truly great actress, she has the capacity of making herself suggest a vision of sheer beauty when the drama demands it. With the play of a smile in the corner of her lips, the erect carriage of a regal figure, the electricity of her eyes, she seems, indeed—when Siegfried inspires her with love—a goddess become woman!

Flagstad's phenomenal success in New York aroused no little skepticism across the ocean. In 1936, she received an invitation to give several guest performances at Covent Garden, London. That England did not take this American discovery very seriously became apparent with Flagstad's first appearance. She sang Isolde on May 18, 1936, receiving a handsome response from the audience. The critics admitted they had been suspicious of her fame in America, but were now glad to acclaim her as a great

Lauritz Melchior
in Tristan und Isolde

artist. From that moment on, Flagstad's popularity in London has been almost as great as it has been in America.

In Vienna, where she appeared for the first time on September 2, 1936, her success was immediate. She had been engaged somewhat grudgingly. To some of the directors of the Vienna State Opera, the importation of a new Wagnerian soprano from New York to Vienna was strangely reversing the process of several decades ("Anny Konetzni," they said, "is good enough for us!"). Pressure, however, was brought to bear on the recalcitrant directors, and Flagstad was invited. Once she emerged on the stage as Isolde, her acceptance by the Viennese music public was whole-hearted. "The stunning thing about this Isolde . . . is the way she sings," wrote one critic in Vienna. "The tone is wholly effortless, wholly 'forward,' wholly soaring, floating from her mouth as easily as a leaf floats from a tree."

5

If, as an intimate friend of Flagstad, you were permitted to be with her a great part of the time, you would justifiably question the novels and moving pictures which enshroud the life of a prima donna in glamour. There is little of the aura of glamour about Flagstad's daily routine. It is systematically routinized. She arises early, awakened by her masseuse who puts her body through a rigorous work-out. After a sparing breakfast, which consists of nothing more than grapefruit juice, Flagstad spends the rest of the morning in complete relaxation, if there is no rehearsal at the Metropolitan. She enjoys a cocktail before lunch, preferably a dry Martini. If her favorite dishes are served, the main course of her lunch will be either fish pudding with lobster sauce or broiled chicken.

The afternoons are spent either in relaxation, or in rehearsal at the Metropolitan, or in private study of her rôles. The evenings on which there is no opera scheduled are spent quietly, sometimes alone with books, her correspondence, or knitting; sometimes in the company of a few select friends. Flagstad almost never attends parties, elaborate functions, or night clubs. Gambling, or imbibing of liquor in great quantities, bore her. If it is the evening of the opera, she will compensate herself with a half bottle of champagne when the performance is over. Then she will go to her hotel suite and spend a quiet hour playing solitaire—to permit, as she herself has put it, the music of the evening to leave her consciousness completely.

During the summer months of vacation, life for Flagstad is as systematic and uneventful. She spends her sum-

mer with her husband, her daughter, and her three step-
children on her beautiful estate in Kristiansand on the
North Sea. Here, her principal diversions are swimming
and the care of the rock garden. Vocal exercises are rarely
pursued; about the only serious singing in which Flagstad indulges during these vacation weeks is at four
o'clock in the afternoon when she prefaces her husband's
afternoon nap with one or two well loved songs.

There are holidays in the winter, too. Her difficult
schedule is always interrupted in mid-winter to give her
a breathing spell. At such times, she takes extended skiing
or hunting trips with her husband. During these trips,
Flagstad does her own cooking. Her specialty is meat-
balls with mushrooms, but only because she does not
know how to cook anything else. Meat-balls and mushrooms is, therefore, the exclusive fare of Flagstad and
her husband during these winter expeditions.

As a friend, you would find her gracious, lovable, soft
of nature, and easy to get along with. She does not tax
your friendship with a volatility of mood. On the contrary, she is remarkably equable of temperament, almost
never yielding to those tempests which story books per-
petually ascribe to the prima donna. At rehearsals she is
pliable and even-tempered, capable of working hard and
open to all suggestions and advice. As in the opera house,

so in her everyday life: her nerves are like steel, and nothing short of a volcano can upset her. She literally glows with mental and physical health.

You would also find her to be an essentially simple and undemanding person. Her needs are few. She detests display or ornamentation of any kind. She dislikes having servants or maids helping her in anything. She always does her own packing, answers her own correspondence, and attends to the details of dress herself. Even at the opera house she dislikes any help in the application of make-up.

What she considers the two greatest events of her spectacular career in America give, probably, an insight into the simplicty of her character. Included among these two unforgettable experiences will not be found her American début, when she suddenly emerged from obscurity to world fame, or her first appearance in New York as Isolde when she was cheered by a rapturous audience. Her two great American experiences are made of other stuff. The first of these took place in Detroit, when her automobile was escorted by policemen on motorcycles, and shrieking sirens, from the General Motors broadcast to the railroad station. That incident thrilled her as no triumph in the opera house. The other was at a flower show in New York, where they named an amaryllis after her. "I was never quite so touched in my life," she said simply.

Her phenomenal fame in the opera house has somewhat thrown into a shade her equally successful career in the concert hall. She fulfills from fifty to sixty concert engagements each year, and has visited almost all of the principal cities in this country. Her art, in song, is no less profound nor less moving than it is in opera, and she is rapidly being accepted by the world as one of the great living artists of song today.

V: MELCHIOR

CHAPTER FIVE

LAURITZ MELCHIOR

LAURITZ MELCHIOR began his artistic career as a second-rate baritone of Italian operas. But he brought it to a culmination as the greatest German tenor of our time.

This transition from one range of voice to another—and coincidentally from mediocrity to greatness—was effected through the astuteness of a woman, a famous American contralto, Mme. Charles Cahier. On April 2, 1913, at the Copenhagen Royal Opera, Melchior made his début as Silvio in *Pagliacci*. Following several subsequent operatic appearances he made an extensive concert tour through Sweden as Count Luna in *Il Trovatore*, with Mme. Cahier as prima donna.

It was during these appearances with Mme. Cahier—a musician of extraordinary discernment—that she noticed the unusually soft texture of Melchior's voice and the flexibility of his high tones. These vocal qualities of Melchior suggested to her the possibility that Melchior might have placed his voice in the wrong range, that, consequently, he was not being heard to best advantage.

She suggested that he attempt a readjustment of voice.

This was no small decision for Melchior to make. It meant the immediate desertion of concert work, and the return to several additional years of arduous vocal exercises. It meant also the acquisition of a completely new operatic repertoire. But Melchior had faith in Mme. Cahier's judgment. He decided to follow her suggestion. That decision changed his artistic destiny—and gave us our greatest Tristan and Siegfried since Jean de Reszke.

A second fortuitous influence brought Melchior from Italian to German opera. On October 8, 1918, Melchior made his return début, this time as Tannhäuser in Copenhagen. This début was only moderately successful, and other engagements were not plentiful. The following year, a friend invited him to London where he was at once engaged as a soloist with the Queen's Hall orchestra, directed by Sir Henry J. Wood. In the audience was the celebrated English novelist, Hugh Walpole. Walpole, moved by a certain human quality in Melchior's voice, decided to make contact with the singer and place at his disposal the resources of his influence, advice and financial assistance for the advancement of his career. It was Walpole who urged Melchior to study the German language and to essay the more important Wagnerian tenor rôles.

Once again permitting himself to be influenced by good advice, Melchior left for Germany and became a student of Frau Anna Bahr-Mildenburg (the celebrated Wagnerian soprano of Bayreuth and Vienna). Under her tutelage, he received stringent and rigorous training in Wagnerian traditions. For months, hour after hour, he sang for her the rôle of Siegmund, as she analyzed for him each phrase and tried to instil in him a coherent conception of the rôle. Not until she was completely satisfied with the results of her comprehensive instruction did she permit Melchior to make his Wagnerian début. This took place on May 14, 1924 in Covent Garden when Melchior appeared as Siegmund in *Die Walküre* with Bruno Walter conducting.

And what a dramatic début that was for the new Wagnerian heroic tenor! At that time Covent Garden was absorbed with a forthcoming production of Strauss' *Der Rosenkavalier*—so absorbed that it completely forgot the fact that a new tenor was making his début in *Die Walküre*. Negligently, the necessary rehearsals for Melchior were not called. At the last moment the directors of Covent Garden were faced with the terrifying prospect of a novice appearing without the benefit of a single rehearsal! Desperately, Bruno Walter cried that Melchior must not be permitted to appear, that a substitute must be called. A substitute, at this last moment, was not available. Resigned to a terrible fate, Walter permitted Melchior to make an appearance. After the performance, Walter rushed backstage and warmly congratulated Melchior. Without a single rehearsal, he had made his début as Siegmund with the utmost of confidence and poise!

Two months later, on July 23, 1924, Melchior appeared in Bayreuth for the first time, as Parsifal, with Dr. Karl Muck conducting.

His ascent to recognition was now swift. The Metropolitan Opera House—its Wagnerian repertory oppressed for many years by inadequate German tenors—was eagerly searching the European horizon for promising material. Melchior had shown enough promise to be engaged for the following season.

On the afternoon of February 17, 1926, Melchior stepped for the first time on the stage of the Metropolitan Opera House in the title rôle of *Tannhäuser*.

It cannot be said that his first appearance at the Metropolitan Opera House was in the nature of a historic triumph. His introduction to America took place on the same day of the blatantly publicized début of an American soprano, Marion Talley. The newspapers found in this Kansas City girl much grist for their journalistic mill, and exploited her fully. A carefully planned publicity campaign, on the part of the Metropolitan itself, assisted in converting what might have otherwise been a humdrum début into an event of national importance. Months before her appearance, Marion Talley's simple mid-Western origin was converted by the press into a saga of a native American singer. News items poured from the presses about her background and training; her sudden emergence from obscurity to fame was dramatized. A few days before her début, the news columns described the special delegation of home-town folk which had come from Kansas City to attend the première of its native daughter; much was made of the fact that Talley's father, a telegraph operator, would send to the world his impressions of his daughter's début over a special wireless set rigged up backstage.

The garish limelight of attention had been focused so strongly on the début of the new American soprano from the mid-West that, inevitably, the introduction of a new German tenor that very same afternoon passed in almost complete darkness. Few of the first string critics of the New York papers were present to pass judgment. The afternoon passed by silently without drawing much attention or praise to the new importation.

But even if the major critics had been present, it is doubtful if they would have recognized in the Tannhäuser of that afternoon the promise of greatness to come. That afternoon Melchior's voice had a warm and pleasant quality which set it apart from that of other German tenors of the Metropolitan—Rudolf Laubenthal or Kurt Taucher, for example. But it appeared to be a limited voice, at best, which—though manipulated intelligently —was incapable of mastering the intricacies or exacting demands of Wagnerian style. Moreover, on the stage Melchior moved somewhat stiffly and uneasily. The best that could be said of his Tannhäuser that day was that it was a mannered and self-conscious characterization.

Melchior's career in New York was not destined to be marked by a sudden flight to fame with one performance, or even with one season of performances. His art developed slowly—evolved, changed, grew, and then burst into full maturity during several seasons of uninterrupted singing on the Metropolitan stage. During these years, his voice became strengthened and enriched. Its fiber acquired both sensitivity and strength, pliancy and resilience. He acquired stage poise, learned how to make each gesture telling and effective with economy of movements. His interpretation of the great Wagnerian tenor rôles became integrated, drawn intelligently even in minute details, a complete and unified artistic conception. Gradually Melchior's art grew on the audiences of the Metropolitan until, almost without their being aware of when or how it happened, he appeared to them suddenly the long-awaited answer to the most pressing need of the Metropolitan Opera House, a German tenor

who combined a magnificent voice with a stage presence
that commanded respect and admiration.

2

Lauritz Lebrecht Hommel Melchior was born in
Copenhagen on March 20, 1890, the descendant of a
long line of educators and clergymen, two of whom had
been founders and leaders of the Melchior School for
Boys, famous throughout all of Denmark. He was the
youngest of six children, one of whom—his best loved
sister, Agnes—was born blind.

The family was left orphaned while Lauritz was an
infant. The care of both the household and the children
was entrusted to Froeken Kristine Jensen, who proved to
be as industrious and solicitous a housekeeper as she was
a genius in the art of cooking (she was the author of many
famous Jensen cook books). She looked after the children
—Lauritz particularly—with the solicitude of a mother.
Each morning she dressed Lauritz and prepared him for
the Melchior School; each Sunday morning she personally conducted him to the English Church where he
served as a choir boy. It was as a choir boy that he first
attracted attention to his voice. The Danish Princess
Alexandria, who was then Queen of England, visited
Copenhagen and attended the English Church. The

Princess singled out Melchior for praise, patting his head and prophesying a great future for him.

His first important musical influence was the opera. His sister Agnes—being blind—was permitted to attend the Royal Opera regularly, seated in a special section under the stage reserved for blind students. Agnes had her brother accompany her to each performance. Wide-eyed he watched the world of illusion unfold before him, as the music poured opulently into his ears. Those operas made an unforgettable impression on him. He could not remove the vivid scenes from his mind, or forget the gorgeous music. Before long he began to disturb his father, for he wanted to study singing seriously; he wanted to become an opera singer.

Money was not plentiful in the Melchior household, and without money an intensive music education for Lauritz seemed impossible. Froeken Kristine Jensen, the housekeeper, whose success with her cook books brought her a comfortable bank account, supplied the money necessary for Lauritz's education. This money opened for Lauritz the doors of the Royal Opera House School in 1912, an apprentice school for the opera house, in which the student was subjected to training in every branch of the operatic and dramatic art. A year of study brought Melchior from the school to the opera company itself. He was chosen to take the place of a baritone who

had left the company for Germany. Then a series of fortuitous circumstances already described brought him
from baritone to tenor voice, and from the Italian repertory to the German.

The year of his Metropolitan Opera House début
was preceded, a year earlier, by another all-important
event in Melchior's life. Maria Haaker, a well-known
German movie star (often referred to as the Mary Pick-
ford of Germany) made a parachute jump from a plane
while filming a picture. The wind blew her off her course,
and brought her into the backyard of Melchior's house
near Munich, almost into his very arms. The romance
that followed culminated with marriage on May 26,
1925. Shortly after their marriage, *"Kleinchen"* (as
Melchior affectionately calls her) resigned from her
motion-picture work to become her husband's secretary,
business manager and adviser. Several times she has been
offered tempting movie contracts from Hollywood to
return to the screen, but always she has remained firm in
her decision that her only career remain that of admin-
istering to the needs and comforts of her celebrated husband.

Since his Metropolitan Opera House début of 1926,
Melchior has made history as the greatest Wagnerian
tenor of our time. He has sung the rôle of Tristan more
than one hundred and fifty times (his foremost predeces-

sor, Jean de Reszke, had sung Tristan less than fifty times), in sixteen different opera houses and under twenty-two different conductors, including Toscanini. On February 22, 1935, there was commemorated the one hundredth performance of his Siegfried. In honor of this event, Melchior was presented with a sword, to be used in all future Siegfried performances, forged after an old Viking sword in the Metropolitan Museum of Art by Kenneth Lynch, a famous New York metal craftsman. The presentation was made on the stage of the Metropolitan Opera House after the performance by George Beck, the Danish consul-general, in the presence of Gatti-Casazza, manager of the Metropolitan, and the Honorable Fiorello H. La Guardia, Mayor of New York.

3

In Siegfried, Melchior has found the rôle in which to unfold his personality most completely. Here, perhaps, lies the secret of the incomparable authenticity and richness of his characterization. Off the stage of the opera house, he is Siegfried to the life, a heroic figure standing six feet three in his stockinged feet, two hundred and fifty pounds of muscle and sinew. The size of his collar is eighteen, and his shoes are a size twelve. Yet the impression he gives is not that of oversize but of prodigious strength .

"*Kleinchen*" has frequently described how Melchior, in Siegfried manner, likes to walk through the woods and listen to the singing of birds. And like Siegfried he is capable of athletic action as well as quiet revery. Melchior's favorite diversion (once again he is Siegfried to the life!) is hunting. Each year, when the opera season is over, he sets off on a long and extensive hunting expedition. The pelts of his victims become the skins he wears for his warrior rôles. He keeps an accurate and comprehensive log of every hunting trip, every killing he makes, every experience he encounters. As you look through this book you will learn that at one time he and a company of friends shot 368 pheasants, wild boars and other game in one trip, and that more recently he himself felled a six hundred pound bear in the Canadian shooting hide-out of Richard Crooks, the tenor. You would also learn that, in 1935, he almost met death. He was hunting wild pigs in South America when, turning around in a brush, he confronted a panther rushing at him. It required coolness of head, sureness of trigger finger and accuracy of aim to save him from certain annihilation. The skin of the panther is now worn by Mrs. Melchior as a coat. Recently he shot a mighty 1,600 pound American bison.

Seeking an apt word with which to describe Melchior you inevitably come upon "expansiveness." As his physique, so his daily habits. Whatever he does is done on a Gargantuan scale. When he travels, it is with twenty-two trunks, and sometimes with five dogs. A meal for him is a prodigious feast including appetizer, soup, beefsteak, potatoes, vegetables, salad, dessert, coffee, a quart of burgundy wine, and a big Havana cigar. Beer he drinks in vast quantities when his day of work is over. When he wishes to walk, it is frequently a twenty-five mile hike. When he prepares a snack of *Smorgasbord* for his guests —a rite which he performs once each year on his birthday—it comprises no less than one hundred and fifty varieties of food. A bridge game in which he indulges becomes an all-night session.

Expansive, too, is the number of his diversions and pastimes. Hunting, fishing, hiking are some of his outdoor sports; indoors, he finds equal pleasure in playing bridge, boxing, cooking (his *specialité de la maison* is an ox-tail soup which takes him two days to prepare), mixing luscious "fruit-bowles," modeling opera characters in almond paste which he sends to friends for Christmas. He is also a rabid collector of curiosities and stamps.

His flair for expansiveness is visible in his home. It is a 3,000 acre estate in Chossewitz, Germany, fifty-five miles southeast of Berlin. The vast lands are heavily populated by deer, rabbit, partridges, pheasants, elks and wild boars. The main house, three stories tall, comprises more than twenty rooms. It is surrounded by beautiful formal gardens. The terrace where the family frequently gathers for its meals, overlooks a spacious lake at the bottom of the hill, fronted by a picturesque Tyrolean boathouse. Melchior's home gives the impression of vastness, immensity.

At the well-crowded dinner table on the terrace will be found not only Melchior, *"Kleinchen,"* their son, Ib and daughter, Birte, but also Melchior's blind sister, Agnes (who now heads a school for the blind in Copenhagen), the mother of *"Kleinchen,"* and any number of personal friends—possibly Hugh Walpole, Jean Hersholt, Lotte Lehmann, Richard Crooks, Capt. Peter Freuchen, all of whom visit Melchior frequently.

Deriving as he does such a keen pleasure from prying in dusty corners of old shops and purchasing handfuls of antiques, Melchior's home is something of an old curiosity shop in itself. In every corner and on every available shelf can be found artistic odds-and-ends. Pieces of baroque art (Melchior's favorite) are to be found at the side of old oriental porcelains and art pieces. Silk damasks, historic in age, cover the walls. Somewhere in the house will be found a unique collection of grandfather clocks, a whole room once the property of the baroque

Church in Trier, and a mirror once the personal possession of Bismarck.

Within the setting of his luxurious estate, Melchior is
informal and unpretentious—frequently dressed in the
leather breeches, feather cap and woolen hose of the
Tyrolean peasant. While roaming about the countryside
of Chossewitz he is frequently mistaken for a peasant.
More than once, when stopped by a visitor for directions,
has he been compensated for his help with a ten *pfennig*
coin!

He is usually in good spirits, enjoys a good story bois-
terously, and usually indulges playfully in schoolboy
pranks, particularly on his wife.

One of the curious qualities in his nature is a strong
vein of vanity. He derives a genuine thrill from appearing at social functions in full dress attire, with his many
decorations suspended from his breast. And innumerable
have been the public honors bestowed upon him! Upon
him has been conferred the Knighthood of Denneborg,
the Knighthood of Bulgaria, the Saxonian Order of
Knights and the French Legion of Honor. He has been
appointed by the King of Denmark "Singer to the Danish Court." He has received the Silver Cross of Denmark
and the *"Ingenio et Arti,"* which has been given only to
three men—the leading actor, poet and singer of the
country. He has also received the Carl Eduard Medal,

first class, from Sachen Coburg Gotha, for his outstanding service at Bayreuth.

He is not usually very sensitive or easily inflamed to
anger. But for some inexplicable reason, he is excessively
vulnerable about his name. To have it misspelled or mis-
pronounced makes his eyes bulge and his face burn with
uncontrolled fury. Much to his credit, he has the humor
to laugh at his own weakness. For a long time he carried
with him a printed card which he immediately gave to
the one who abused his name. It read:

> "There is a tenor big and jolly,
>   Who's hardly ever melancholy,
>   There's just one thing that can raise his ire,
>   To have his name misspelled Melchoir.
>   Such carelessness will bring a roar
>   Of rage, from Lauritz Melchior!"

VI: HOFMANN

CHAPTER SIX

JOSEF HOFMANN

WHEN on the evening of November 28, 1937, Josef Hofmann gave his golden jubilee concert at the Metropolitan Opera House, there must have been more than one in the audience whose memory could reach back fifty years. Then, in that very same hall, Hofmann made his American début—a child prodigy. That début had been one of the great events, not only in the musical but also in the social life of New York during the closing decades of the nineteenth century. He was, at the time, eleven years old. His early photographs reveal a round face with small features, his closely cropped hair encircling his head like a tight skull cap. His nose was turned slightly upwards over lips that were thin and fine; his eyes were soft and sensitive; his hands, small but strong. There was nothing effete about him. His chubby cheeks radiated health, while his body showed muscle and sinew.

He had come to America with news of an almost incredible career preceding him, a career extravagantly discussed in the newspapers and magazines before his

109

arrival, and talked about over tea cups and liquor glasses in the nation's living rooms. He was the "musical phenomenon" as Anton Rubinstein had referred to him.

His life story, brief though it was at the time, had been well known before he arrived: how, in ten meager years he had crowded enough triumph to enrich many a full life's span. Born in Cracow, Poland, on January 20, 1876, he was the child of musical parents: his mother was an operatic soprano of some renown; his father Casimir, a composer, pianist and a conductor at the Warsaw Opera. Already at the age of three and a half, Josef played upon the piano, taught first by his little sister, a year and a half his senior. Josef learned his exercises with lightning rapidity. He passed from the instruction of his child-sister to that of his aunt; and, one year later —because his aunt could teach him no more—he became a pupil of his father.

A little more than a year after he had first touched the piano, Josef made his professional début in a suburb of Warsaw. It was considered by many a sensational first-performance, so much so that a deluge of offers descended upon Casimir Hofmann to have his son concertize. Wisely, father Hofmann refused to exploit the child. He permitted only a scattered handful of concerts, all for charity—carefully spaced to spare the energies of the child. These concerts spread the boy's reputation throughout Poland.

When he was seven years old, the child played the first movement of Beethoven's first piano concerto with what the critics referred to as an instinctive feeling for the style of the composer, precision, and a full round singing tone. It was about this time that Anton Rubinstein heard him play for the first time, in Warsaw. The performance stirred the master profoundly. He soon spoke about this amazing prodigy to the German impresario, Hermann Wolf, suggesting concert appearances. How deeply Rubinstein had been moved by Hofmann's playing became even more evident a few months later in London. A friend of Rubinstein broached the subject of child prodigies, and Rubinstein said that he had little taste for them. There was only one exception, the master said, the equal of which the history of music would surely fail to duplicate. "And the name of the scoundrel," said Rubinstein, as he struck several powerful chords on the piano, "is Josef Hofmann!"

The impresario, Hermann Wolf, persistently urged Casimir Hofmann to permit concert engagements for the boy. The world of music, he argued, must hear him. When Josef was ten years old, father Hofmann yielded to the entreaties of the manager. Hofmann's first concert out of Poland was in Berlin, at one of the symphony concerts of the Berlin Philharmonic, when he played the complete first piano concerto of Beethoven. His concert was a triumph; the audience cheered its appreciation wildly after the performance. But no less impressed had been the members of the orchestra itself, for, at the first rehearsal, they had witnessed the child Josef pulling the coat of the conductor, Prof. Manstadt, to tell him that the violoncellos were not playing correctly in one passage —a defection which few of the other musicians had noticed!

Appearances followed in Denmark, Sweden, Norway and Holland. From there Hofmann went to Paris where Saint-Saëns exclaimed that this phenomenon had nothing more to learn, that he was the "greatest wonder of the present age."

With all this America was well familiar; long before his much-heralded début in the United States, his exploits were consistently recorded in the press. "For nearly four years he has been appearing before the public as a piano virtuoso," wrote the *Harper's Young People* of 1887, comparing Hofmann to Mozart in an earlier paragraph, "and lately he appeared very frequently, and created what the newspapers call a 'sensation.' Never was so much written about a young man by his contemporaries as has been written about this young Hofmann.

Famous musicians like Rubinstein, and callous old critics like—well, most of the famous ones—have fairly gushed over him. It is a wonder that with all the attention he has received, the little fellow has not become very conceited. . . . Away from music, he is always a child, and his sense of humor is delightful. One day, his parents promised to pay him twenty-five cents for each concert, and subsequently when he finished a concert and encores were demanded, he said: 'No,' with a merry laugh, 'the concert is over and I have earned my quarter.' But he played encores, and upon returning to the artists' room said, 'Now, in the future, you must pay me by the piece—two cents for my own compositions, and five cents for the others.' "

When Josef Hofmann stepped on the stage of the Metropolitan Opera House on November 29, 1887— performing the first piano concerto of Beethoven, the *Variations* by Rameau, a *Polacca* by Weber-Liszt, a set of pieces by Chopin and one of his own creations—the atmosphere was charged with expectancy. A thundering ovation welcomed him as he stepped on the platform, dressed in a striped sailor shirt and knee breeches—a pretty sight for the eye. Then, with poise and self-assurance, he climbed to the stool, ran his fingers casually over the keys, and patiently waited for the whispers and exclamations of the audience to subside. Only when an intense silence prevailed did he signal to the conductor to begin the opening bars of the concerto. Then he played. . . . "When he concluded the Beethoven concerto," reported W. J. Henderson the following morning in the *New York Times*, "a thunder of applause swept through the opera house. Many people leaped to their feet. Men shouted 'Bravo!' and women waved their handkerchiefs. Pianists of repute were moved almost to tears. Some wiped the moisture from their eyes. The child had astonished the assembly. He was a marvel. The second movement of the Beethoven concerto was performed in a manner that startled experienced observers of musical events. The first movement had been played with wonderful refinement of touch, with a complete mastery of technical difficulties, with rich and varied tone, color, and with surprising brilliancy in the treatment of the difficult Moscheles cadenza. But in the second movement there was no room for imposition on the senses through the medium of ornamental passages. The pure and elevated melody stood forth in unclothed beauty, and could only be adequately interpreted by an artist. Josef Hofmann played, not only like an artist, but like a master. The tenderness of sentiment, the poetic insight into the meaning, the symmetrical conception of the movement as a whole, and the ability to make the music not only arouse the intelligence but move the heart of the

Josef Hofmann

hearer, displayed by this child, were simply wonderful. . . . The feeling and intelligence shown by young Hofmann in this movement was far and away beyond his years. They showed that he was a born musician—that rare thing which the world always hungers for and greets with affectionate veneration. Suffice it to say for the present that Josef Hofmann, as a musical phenomenon, is worthy of the sensation which he created. More than that, he is an artist, and we can listen to his music without taking into consideration the fact that he is a child."

2

The memory of many in the audience which heard Josef Hofmann's golden jubilee concert in 1937 must also have brought back to mind vividly an evening eleven years after the début—in 1898—when Hofmann, no longer the child prodigy but now the mature artist, made his American reappearance as a concert pianist, his first appearance in America since his childhood. He had recently emerged from a long period of retirement, which had been devoted to intensive study. After his phenomenal American début at the Metropolitan Opera House, Hofmann gave sixteen additional concerts at the Metropolitan and twenty-four on tour. Then the Society for Prevention of Cruelty to Children, in New York, intervened, condemning Hofmann's extensive concert work as detrimental to his health and growth. The Society issued extensive propaganda for removing the boy from all active concertizing. Their propaganda proved fruitful. Despite the fact that Hofmann had been booked for eighty engagements in America that year, he was suddenly retired. An anonymous patron appeared (he was later identified as Alfred Corning Clark of New York) who offered to provide financially for the child and his family until Josef Hofmann reached his eighteenth birthday; but on one condition alone—that Josef be kept permanently from the concert stage and be directed only toward study and relaxation.

What followed was a long period of training in which young Hofmann was given thorough and comprehensive schooling not only in music but in academic subjects as well. The family returned to Europe where the study of musical theory and composition was pursued under Heinrich Urban, and the piano first under Casimir Hofmann and then under Moritz Moszkowski. Moszkowski was no less enthusiastic about his pupil than other teachers had been. "The boy knows so much," he once said, "and plays so much better than I do, that I don't know how to teach him."

When Josef Hofmann reached his sixteenth birthday, he became the only private pupil of Anton Rubinstein.

He had long wished to study under Rubinstein, but the master—despite his one-time enthusiasm for Hofmann's genius—remained obstinate in his refusal to accept private pupils. At a party in Berlin, given by the impresario Hermann Wolf and at which Rubinstein was a guest, Hofmann was invited to play. He performed his own *Theme, Variations and Fugue,* Opus 14. After the performance Rubinstein approached him. "You may not be a pianist yet," he said, "but you are certainly a musician." Lukewarm praise, it seemed. But how deeply Rubinstein had actually been moved by Hofmann's music was forcibly demonstrated then and there when the master decided to accept Hofmann as his only private pupil.

Teaching Hofmann was for Rubinstein an experience which brought with it renewed reward and cause for wonder; Rubinstein never wearied in relating the wonders of his phenomenal pupil. "He is," said the master—who was never careless with superlatives, particularly where the playing of the piano was concerned, "the greatest genius of music the world has ever known."

One day (Hofmann had by this time been Rubinstein's pupil for two years) the master called his pupil and ordered him to commit to memory and prepare for concert performance within two days the D-minor concerto of Rubinstein. Hofmann, terrified, exclaimed that two days was too short a time for such a formidable assignment. "Formidable?" answered Rubinstein. "There is *nothing* formidable for us!"

Two days later Hofmann had learned the concerto. That very evening at a symphony concert in Hamburg he made his first appearance on the concert stage in seven years. At the end of the performance, Rubinstein rushed to the stage and threw his huge arms about his pupil. For that performance had proved to Rubinstein that Hofmann was in consummate command of all the resources of the piano, that he had become a mature and profound artist, prepared for his life as a concert pianist.

Six months later, in the autumn of 1894, a new extensive tour was launched by Hofmann, first in England (where his audience included his benefactor, Alfred Corning Clark, who had come from America expressly to attend that performance), and then Germany and Russia. In 1898, Hofmann crossed the Atlantic westwards for a second time, and in a tour which brought him from one coast to another, demonstrated eloquently to audiences that crowded the concert halls to the doors that the one-time prodigy had grown into one of the great artists of his time.

Meanwhile, Hofmann had said permanent farewell to his master Rubinstein, who had been such a profound influence upon his artistic growth. Their last musical association had taken place in Hamburg in March of 1894, when Hofmann played the Rubinstein D-minor concerto with the composer conducting. A few weeks later—following a Rubinstein concert in Leipzig which Hofmann attended—a social tea brought teacher and pupil together for the last time. "When will you listen to me play again?" Hofmann asked Rubinstein. "Never again!" bellowed the great Russian master. "I have told you all I know myself about piano playing. If you do not know how to play yet, you can go to hell!"

Hofmann was never again to play for his teacher. On November 19, 1894, Hofmann traveled from London to Cheltenham when a newspaper headline announced to him that Rubinstein was dead. "It seemed to me that I had not only lost my greatest benefactor but also the dearest person on earth, for not only did I admire him, I had grown to love him as well."

By a curious coincidence, Hofmann was scheduled to play that evening, at his concert in Cheltenham, the great B-flat minor Sonata of Chopin, with the funeral march. That evening he played the funeral march not for his audience but for the great master who had died that day. Never before, and perhaps never since, had he so poured his heart into this music which was his tribute to Rubinstein. The audience must have sensed the significance of Hofmann's performance. One by one they stood up, as Hofmann was playing, and during the closing page the entire audience was on its feet, its head bowed reverently. The audience, too, was paying its last tribute to Rubinstein.

3

Hofmann has enriched the art of music through more than one channel. He has been a composer of many works which, if not of Gargantuan stature, are not by any means insignificant. Until 1922, Hofmann disguised his work created in the modern vein under the pseudonym of "Michel Dvorsky"—so that his enormous fame as a virtuoso might not influence the music world on behalf of his creations. For years, "Michel Dvorsky"—the ghost of Hofmann—haunted the concert halls. Piano pieces by this unknown name were introduced at recitals by leading virtuosos; a symphonic poem and other larger compositions for orchestra, or orchestra and piano, were performed by symphony organizations. And for years the world at large remained ignorant of the true identity of Dvorsky. It was rumored that Dvorsky was a new Russian composer residing in Spain; more than that nothing was known. Finally Hofmann revealed himself. As though to commemorate the liberation, an entire Josef Hofmann program was featured by the Philadelphia Symphony Orchestra on January 2, 1924. It included the symphonic poem *The Haunted Castle*, the second Concerto for piano and orchestra, and *Chromaticon*, a "symphonic dialogue for piano and orchestra."

Even more significant has been Hofmann's rôle as a teacher. In 1926, Hofmann was appointed the director of the Curtis School of Music in Philadelphia. During the twelve years in which he directed one of the great Conservatories in this country, his influence was felt by a rising generation of young pianists. Unfortunately, in 1938, Hofmann decided that his day as a teacher and director was over. He was eager to extend his concert work, to compose more extensively, and, possibly, to record on phonograph discs his major performances. His withdrawal as director of the Curtis School has removed one of the major musical influences in our country.

Yet—distinguished though his work as composer and teacher may be—his greatest importance rests on his piano playing. So much has been written about Hofmann's technical capacities that detailed comment should be unnecessary here. Certainly, his digital equipment for the piano is breath-taking: his complete control of all the resources of the piano, from the sensitivity of whispering voices to the full-throated sonority of orchestral chords. Certainly few in our time can enunciate, as Hofmann can, scale passages with such crystalline clarity, cleanliness and despatch; and few have his remarkably infallible instinct for the rhythmic beat. Certainly, too, few pianists of our experience can convert the piano into such a choir of singing strings as Hofmann can: his tone has depth and roundness, intensity and warmth, variety of color and delicacy of tints. He is the complete master of the keyboard; the instrument is utterly at his command, and all music is under his hands immaculately, perfectly conceived.

Such a phenomenal command of his instrument Hofmann had when Rubinstein lavished his adulation upon him; and such a phenomenal command he still possesses. And with this equipment, which some go so far as to say is without comparison in our time, he brings—in the performance of certain works—a fullness of heart, a breadth of conception, a living force, a windswept emotion, a beauty of design and expression which make him one of the great interpreters of our generation.

4

The critics have incessantly spoken of the eternal youth in Hofmann's playing. Youth, indeed—for youth has never forsaken Hofmann himself. The exhausting and strenuous life of a world famous concert artist has exacted small penalty from him. Most concert artists, when they pass their sixtieth birthday, appear excessively aged, their energies sapped, their physical appearance weatherbeaten by the strain and stress of endless travel and concert appearances. But there is still something remarkably youthful and fresh about Hofmann.

He has even retained remarkably the features of his boyhood: the round face and chubby cheeks, the closely cropped hair, the upturned nose, the small, powerful hands. His skin is still soft and supple, and remarkably free of the lines and creases of age; wrinkles on his face appear only when he smiles—short lines which converge from his eyes, giving his face not a little of its engaging charm. But he has retained not only the features, but even the extraordinary energy and health of his youth. Today he appears amazingly vital. Athletics—boating and hiking particularly—have kept his body resilient and strong. When he shakes your hand, you hold a firm, strong grasp. His gestures, which are frequent, are animated. When he talks, it is always volubly and energetically (his conversation liberally studded with epigrams) —so zestfully that, after a few sentences, he must stop for a fraction of a second to moisten his lips with the tip of his tongue, which he does with flashing rapidity.

An amazing variety of interests has kept his spirit as vigorous and young as his body. Music is only one major element of a well-proportioned existence. It has not interfered with an intelligent and satisfying home life. Hofmann, in spite of extensive concert tours, knows a very retiring domestic life at his spacious home in Merion, Pennsylvania, where he lives the greater part of the year with his wife and three sons. Here he finds relaxation in playing ping-pong, rummy, or chess with his boys. Here, too, he absorbs himself with his one major hobby, which has fascinated him since boyhood—invention and mechanics. When, as a boy, he was forbidden by his mother to ice-skate, he invented a collapsible set which he could conceal in his pockets until he had passed out of his mother's vision. Since that time, he has spent endless hours in the laboratory translating what might first have appeared as fantastic dreams into practical realities. He was the first to design a model house, the foundation of which is capable of rotating with the sun. When steam-cars came into fashion, Hofmann built one for himself which he used for his personal transportation around the country. The oil-burning furnace in his home was designed and built by him. He has also invented, and built, air-springs for automobile, shock-absorbers and snubbers. To cope with warped floors on concert platforms which caused the piano bench to wobble, he has invented a collapsible bench, the legs of which can be adjusted individually to conform to the elevations or decline in the floor boards.

Where music is concerned, his tastes are amazingly conservative. He has little taste for the modern or the experimental in present-day music, and his concerts avoid the new and unfamiliar almost scrupulously. A Hofmann recital is, for the most part, a voyage on familiar trails— familiar trails on which he points out for us new subtle beauties in the landscape which had formerly eluded us. He has a phenomenal memory for music, can almost impress upon his mind an entire composition after one hearing. Pupils of his have been astounded when—having played for him one of their own compositions—Hofmann, without consulting the music, will play on the piano one passage after another exactly as it was put on paper.

Such a phenomenal memory inevitably reduces the hours of practising at a keyboard. Hofmann practises while lounging in a soft chair, while sprawling in a hammock, while taking walks in the woods, or while riding in trains. He closes his eyes, when he relaxes, and appears to be asleep; but he is, in fact, going over every note, and every nuance, of an entire program. Shortly before a concert Hofmann translates this mental practising into actual tones at the piano, but only when his conception of the music is clearly and forcefully impressed on his mind. Hofmann does not recommend this method for every pianist; it requires an enormous capacity for concentration, a prodigious memory, and a complete self-assurance in one's technical facility.

VII: HEIFETZ

CHAPTER SEVEN

JASCHA HEIFETZ

THE word "Heifetz" does not appear in the English dictionary, but one sometimes wonders if it does not deserve a permanent place there. For musicians and lay-men alike, "Heifetz" has become an eloquent word de-scriptive of the *ne plus ultra* of violin virtuosity. Mothers who raise their children to be prodigies speak of them as "little Heifetzes." Critics employing their most precious superlative on a violinist will write: "He plays like a Heifetz."

Glorification came to Heifetz long ago. His artistic career began sensationally when he was six years old ("What were you before that," once asked the irre-pressible Harpo Marx of Heifetz, "just a bum?") and has continued ever since to amass layer upon layer of triumph. In his thirty and more years of active concertiz-ing, Heifetz has traveled almost a million and a half miles. He has played in every corner of the civilized world, and everywhere he is equally idolized. He has concertized during the days of the great Russian up-heaval, during the Sinn Fein uprisings in Ireland, during an earthquake in Japan and in the midst of Gandhi-troubled Bombay. At the Lewisohn Stadium in New York he performed before one of the largest single audiences ever to witness a concert.

His name is known wherever music is made. Even to those who rarely attend a concert hall, the name of Jascha Heifetz has an aura of magic.

To music lovers, of course, Heifetz has legendary stature. Violinists will tell you that Heifetz is the greatest technician of the violin alive; no one can offer comparison to the cleanliness and despatch with which Heifetz performs even the most uncompromisingly difficult passages. But lovers of great music have long ago learned that Heifetz is not merely the perfect instrumental mechanic. He performs with incomparable insight, with a beautiful sense of style, perfect phrasing and above all else an ability to convey the inmost message of the composer—whether it be works like the great concertos of Beethoven, Brahms and Mendelssohn, the fireworks of Vieuxtemps and Wieniawski, the Romantic effusions of Glazunoff and Tschaikovsky, or such modern masterpieces as the concertos of Elgar, Sibelius and Prokofieff. Lightning infallibility of fingers he has—as has been so greatly publicized. But with it a really profound musicianship and taste, insight and discernment. There will

Jascha Heifetz

be few to deny, I am sure, that he stands with the immortal interpreters of all time.

2

Heifetz has been fed on fame and adulation from earliest childhood. Born in Vilna on February 2, 1901, the son of Ruvin Heifetz, a violinist of a Vilna theatre orchestra, Jascha revealed excessive sensitivity to music at a tender age. It was noticed that when he was only eight months old, his face would shine when his father played a beautiful melody on the violin. But when a dissonance was sounded, the infant's face would reflect actual pain. With the passing of several months, the child showed greater fascination with musical sounds. Almost playfully, Ruvin Heifetz bought his son a one-quarter size violin for his third birthday. What had been intended as a mere toy for a child was soon to become an instrument for serious musical expression. Jascha was given a few elementary lessons by his father, which he learned with such eagerness that he was soon given a systematic course of study.

When Jascha reached his fifth birthday, his talent was so evident that the father felt the responsibility of training a genius too formidable for his own capabilities. He entered Jascha in the Royal School of Music at Vilna, placing him under the instruction of Elias Malkin. One year later, the child was ready for his first concert appearance. In Kovno, he played the violin concerto of Mendelssohn with an aplomb and self-assurance that amazed an audience of one thousand. His tone, though small, was firm and round. His little fingers coped with the technical difficulties of the last movement with bewildering precision. After that, for the following two years, the child was scheduled to give periodic public performances in Russia. Everywhere he was spoken of as the *wunderkind* without equal, a phenomenon of nature, a human miracle, to so speak.

It was as a wonder-boy that he made his never-to-be-forgotten American début at Carnegie Hall on October 27, 1917, and it was as a wonder-boy that he then achieved a triumph which only a handful of concert artists of our generation have equaled. Music lovers in the audience were overwhelmed by the exhibition; critics sang paeans of praise; and violinists were dumbfounded. A famous anecdote has it that Leopold Godowsky, the pianist, and Mischa Elman, the violinist, were seated in a box at the concert. During the intermission, Elman made what he thought an innocent remark. "Terribly hot, isn't it?" he asked Godowsky. "Not for pianists," was Godowsky's annihilating retort.

A few years ago—in the spring of 1934—Heifetz was given a rousing welcome when, after seventeen years of absence, he returned to his native country for a series of concerts. Musicians came from as far as Siberia for his first concert. People sold clothing and furniture to obtain the price of admission for one of his performances. Crowds of people stood on the streets, outside the concert hall, shouting their praise. "That," Heifetz has said, "was the greatest emotional experience of my life."

3

When Heifetz was eight years old, he came into contact with the one who probably exerted the greatest single influence upon his career. Leopold Auer, professor of the violin at St. Petersburg Conservatory of Music, came to Vilna on a concert tour. Malkin, a personal friend of Auer, spoke rapturously to him about his prodigy pupil. He told Auer that Jascha Heifetz had technique and taste comparable to those of a fully mature artist. But Auer was impatient with Malkin's rhapsodies. He had heard *wunderkinder* to a point of satiation; they all bored him. Moreover, at the moment, he was too busy, and physically too fatigued, to listen to a prodigy. Another time, perhaps. . . . But Malkin would not recognize defeat. He begged, then insisted that Auer hear for himself. Finally, Auer relented. Little Jascha, accompanied by his father, appeared before the master and with very little ceremony placed fiddle under chin and despatched the concerto of Mendelssohn and the twenty-fourth caprice of Paganini. And Auer—who had protested his impatience with prodigies—embraced the boy and told him that he had not heard such a performance in a long time. He urged the boy to come to St. Petersburg to become his pupil at the Conservatory.

Father Heifetz sold his belongings, resigned his position at the theater, and brought his boy to St. Petersburg. At first there were disheartening disappointments and obstacles for the Heifetz family. When they came to call on Auer, the professor did not recognize Jascha, and thinking him just another prodigy, refused to open his door to him. When finally Auer recognized Jascha as the wonder child of Vilna, the period for entrance into the Conservatory had passed, and Auer's class was filled to capacity. Auer's influence was brought to bear on the situation, and Heifetz, at long last, was admitted to the Conservatory, permitted to enter the class of Auer's assistant for one term. But—even with these difficulties surmounted—the path did not stretch clear for him. Jews were not permitted permanent residence at St. Petersburg. An exception was made for students at the Conservatory, but no allowance was made for the families of the students. It seemed, at one time, that Ruvin Heifetz would be compelled to return to Vilna, leaving his son alone in St. Petersburg. The director of the Conservatory, however, soon found a solution. He entered father Heifetz, aged 40, as a pupil at the Conservatory!

The obstacles surmounted, Jascha Heifetz proceeded to perfect himself as a violinist. After the first six months at the Conservatory, he became a pupil of Auer. His progress from that time was so rapid as to amaze even a callous professor. Auer freely confessed that he had never had a pupil such as this, who seemed able to do everything with the violin, and always in good taste.

During this period of study under Auer, concert work was not abandoned. The fame of the boy expanded and spread throughout all of Europe. He played at the International Exposition in Odessa, where he was so idolized that a police guard was necessary to protect him from admiring masses. The boy gave a concert in St. Petersburg which inspired nothing short of thunderous acclaim. There were appearances in Austria and Germany as well. Whenever he played, critics said that Heifetz the boy was already a full grown artist, and among the greatest. When, in 1914, Heifetz performed at the concerts of the Berlin Philharmonic, the conductor of the orchestra, the incomparable Artur Nikisch, said that he had never before heard such violin playing.

Two years later, in the company of Professor Auer, Heifetz went to Christiania (now Oslo), where once again he became a public idol, performing before royalty, pampered and petted wherever he went. His travels continued—to Japan, by way of Siberia, and then to the United States.

And on October 27, 1917, the wonder-boy of the violin gave his first American concert at Carnegie Hall. His program featured the *Chaconne* of Vitali, the D-minor concerto of Wieniawski, the twenty-fourth caprice of Paganini, and morsels (such as the Schubert-Wilhelmj *Ave Maria,* and the Beethoven-Auer *March* from the *Ruins of Athens*) which have since become inextricably associated with his name.

How triumphant his début was can most accurately be gauged by the ecstasy of the music critics. They had witnessed a phenomenon which had startled and electrified them. They did not mince words. "He is a modern miracle," wrote Pitts Sanborn; "he is a perfect violinist," reported Sigmund Spaeth. "He rose above his instrument and the music written for it," commented H. E. Krehbiel. "This modern young Orpheus seems to do all the things with a violin which a fabled charmer accomplished with a lyre," wrote Leonard Liebling. "He remains unapproached with the perfection of his finger and bow manipulation, the refined wistfulness of his tone, and the unique appeal of his apparently impersonal relation to his playing." And Herbert F. Peyser: "The newcomer plays with a tone so lustrous and silken, so fragrant, so intoxicatingly sweet that only the molten gold of Fritz Kreisler can be conjured up in comparison. But though it wrings the tears from the eyes by its lambent beauty, its vibrancy and infinite play of magical color, its nature bespeaks a singular aristocratic purity rather than an unrelieved sensuousness, though its power of emotional conveyance and suggestion is unparalleled."

4

For the next few years, the stature of Heifetz dominated the concert world. He concertized more extensively than any other living artist, and his following everywhere was fabulous. His earnings at the box office were without equal. He was the magician of the violin, and his audience came to be enchanted.

But, as the years passed, there was voiced a growing dissatisfaction with Heifetz's playing. He was the perfect mechanic, it was true; the consummate technical master of his instrument. But music was much more than technique or mechanics. Where were the pulse, the heart beat, the warm blood of the concertos of Mendelssohn and Brahms, the deep emotion in the Beethoven Concerto when Heifetz played them? Where, in his music, was there that dissecting analysis, that insight and understanding which one should expect from the playing of a great artist? Some called Heifetz cold, impersonal, too objective. The music he performed, they said, was as cold as a slab of marble, beautifully sculptured, it was true, but with the essential vibrancy of a living organism absent.

The truth was—although it was difficult to recognize it at the time—that Heifetz was undergoing a transition as an artist. He was reacting more and more strongly against the Russian sensuousness, the outpouring of sentiment, the emotional extravagances which were part and parcel of his Auer training. And, in reacting strongly, he had gone to an opposite extreme. Besides, this was for Heifetz a period of difficult emotional adjustment, in the face of which his art suffered inevitably.

But when this transition period was over (and it ended about ten years ago), Heifetz emerged a far greater artist than he had been when he entered it. He was still the wonder-boy of 1917, still the incomparable technician. But, more important, there was now discovered in his playing a richer vein, a deep but controlled emotion, wisdom and mellowness. He no longer "despatched" the great sonatas and concertos of the masters. They were now reborn and revitalized under his fingers—as all great music is when it passes through the hands of a great and sensitive artist.

5

In his youth, his thick crop of hair clustered over his brow, his long, lean face and slight build were his identifying trade-marks of an artist. Today, there is little in his appearance which conforms to the traditional conception of the musician. His hair is clipped short, and is combed back neatly. His face has assumed a roundness of contour. The nose descends sharply from a high forehead and overlooks lips that are thin and sensitive. His physique is muscular and resilient, revealing the discipline which comes from a life devoted to boating, swimming, ball playing, wood chopping. His dress is always meticulously correct, whether he is indulging in outdoor sport or is entertaining guests in his living room. His fabulous wardrobe, as a matter of fact, has long been a subject of gentle ridicule among his artist friends.

In 1928, Heifetz married the beautiful Florence Vidor of Hollywood. Together with their children, Josepha and Robert, and their hounds, Roy and Michael, they occupy two residences. One of these is a comfortable, rambling cottage in Balboa, California. The other is a typical New England farmhouse near Norwalk, Connecticut, seventy miles from New York.

The keynotes of his home are simplicity and good taste. There is no excess ornamentation, no ostentatious display of wealth. The furniture, grouped around a fireplace, has dignity as well as comfort. Books, music, phonograph records, original paintings set the tone of culture. To a large degree, the comfortable unpretentiousness of their home reflects the nature of its owners. The members of the Heifetz family are essentially simple people, who enjoy the open country life with an almost peasant lustiness. The Connecticut hills, particularly in the winter when they are covered with snow, offer them far greater satisfaction than night clubs. Hikes or gardening delight them much more than elaborate cocktail parties. Heifetz enjoys drinking in moderation—particularly Connecticut applejack; and he likes to give parties. But in everything he does he has a healthy balance and moderation. He has little use for excesses of any kind.

When he gives a party it is usually a musicale—intimate concerts of chamber music in which Heifetz joins other distinguished musicians. That is his greatest pleasure, opens for him a different world of music than that which is his as a virtuoso. Away from music, Heifetz enjoys good literature (he reads voraciously, and is a collector of books—once, of rare editions), and great painting (he is a friend of Diego Rivera, and a sponsor of Gregory Gluckmann).

The simpler pleasures complete a full life: ping-pong, which he plays extraordinarily well; walks with his children; the camera, his favorite hobby since boyhood; gardening, in which he indulges zestfully, with no attempt at pampering his precious hands.

Sometimes, when a temporary depression of spirit sets in, he finds relaxation and escape in a long drive through country roads. In his driving, as in almost everything else he does, he is more than passingly expert. His two cars bear unique license-plates. The "number" of one of these is "HEI;" the other, "FETZ." These are honorplates which are given to first class drivers and which are revocable at the first transgression of the traffic laws.

In his music, he has the seriousness of purpose, the integrity, the wholesome honesty of the true artist. His recent Hollywood experience is a case in point. When he went to make a picture for Samuel Goldwyn it was only after he had convinced himself that the screen was now capable of excellent musical reproduction; fabulous offers had come to him from Hollywood long before he accepted one. And, in signing his contract with Goldwyn, he insisted upon the right of playing only the greatest in violin literature, and in appearing in the film in no other capacity than that of a concert violinist. His career has been untouched by any opportunism, cheapness, or a debasing of the high artistic standards he has set for himself. Few artists of our time have been so true to themselves and to their profession as Heifetz.

VIII: LEHMANN

CHAPTER EIGHT

LOTTE LEHMANN

A RECEPTION in a New York drawing room. . . .

Rosa Ponselle, famous American singer of the Metropolitan Opera House, is being introduced for the first time to Lotte Lehmann. Impetuously, she throws her arms about Lehmann, kisses her ardently on both cheeks. "Forgive me," she explains simply. "I heard you sing today and I cannot forget how deeply you moved me."

The scene is transferred—to a railroad station of a midwestern American city. Lotte Lehmann, having just finished a recital of songs, is waiting with her accompanist for a midnight train. Only one other person is on the deserted platform—a little man, shivering with the cold. The loneliness of the night, the long wait for the train, and possibly the intensity of his emotions, tempt him to essay conversation with the strangers near him. "Have you, too, heard the recital of Lotte Lehmann tonight?" he asked, oblivious of the identity of the person he was addressing. Before Lehmann could answer, he continued—and his voice quivered as he spoke: "She is the greatest singer on God's earth. I have traveled a hundred miles to hear her. A thousand miles would not have been too great for such a privilege."

Such ecstatic tributes to the art of a singer epitomize to a large extent what the world of music—from the professional musician to the man-of-the-street who, untaught, loves his music instinctively—thinks of Lotte Lehmann.

Though Lehmann may not possess a technical equipment to dazzle and magnetize an audience, the appeal of her art is catholic. Not through gaudy pyrotechnics does Lotte Lehmann capture the adoration of her immense public. As a matter of fact, there are singers, far less famous than she, the range and volume of whose voice is far greater than hers, and who can probably attack a bravura passage with greater sparkle and brilliance. Lehmann has a low register of dark and sensuous beauty, and a *mezza-voce* of enormous effectiveness. But to call hers a great voice, from a technical point of view, would be inaccurate.

And yet, legion is the number that considers her singing one of the great aesthetic experiences which the presentday concert and opera stage has to offer. For Lehmann, whether she sings a *Lied* of Schubert or Hugo Wolf, or etches a characterization of monumental stature such as her Leonore or the Marschallin, brings to the listener an unforgettable emotional experience.

Lotte Lehmann
in Rosenkavalier

LOTTE LEHMANN

Discerning intellect and impeccable taste guide every line of music she sings; often a single phrase is endowed with shattering emotional implications through the most subtle use of shading or nuance. The quality of quiet but heartbreaking pathos with which she endows the closing line of Schubert's *Gretchen am Spinnrade,* the flood of sunlight which she pours into the enchanting phrase *Sonnenschein, O Sonnenschein* by Schumann, the crushing tragedy of her portrait of a beautiful woman grown old in the first act of the *Rosenkavalier* of Richard Strauss —these are only a few of the many great moments which she achieves with passages which, with so many other singers, often become merely perfunctory.

She has conquered two distinct worlds of music, that of the opera and that of the concert stage, each of which requires special aptitude and talent. On the opera stage —not only in the German operas of Beethoven, Wagner and Richard Strauss, but also in the more popular French and Italian repertory—she cuts an imperial figure. The best of her characterizations are etched in large and heroic lines. But her art is by no means cut into one design. One recalls, for example, her performance of the rôle of Christine in Strauss' *Intermezzo* in which she executed a comic part with incomparable nimbleness and grace.

She literally dominates the stage with the magnetism

of her personality. And her voice acquires amplitude, breadth and fullness, together with her acting. On the concert stage—in her inimitable recitals of dramatic songs, or *Lieder*—her style becomes intimate and personalized. She penetrates to the very essence of the poetic message of each song she sings; songs, with Lehmann, become miniature dramas. Yet such is the peculiar quality of her art in her *Lieder* recitals that the listener often acquires the impression of a personal contact with the singer, almost as if Lehmann were singing to him, and to him alone.

Taste, intellect and discernment have frequently been mentioned as qualities of Lehmann's art. Equally important is the fact that whatever Lehmann sings becomes permeated with the warm flush of her personality; and it is this quality, more than any other, which has made an entire music world her admiring public.

Her charm and geniality exert a spell in the opera house and concert hall. In Vienna she has been called the *"geliebte Lehmann"*—"beloved Lehmann." And in other music centers of the world she is esteemed no less affectionately.

Like Kreisler's violin playing, Lehmann's art is Viennese in its charm, grace, zest and warmth of heart.

2

She is essentially a daughter of Vienna, even though her birthplace was Germany. Her appearance is characteristically Viennese. Her figure, her round face, her intelligently expressive eyes, even her manner of wearing her hair (with a part in the middle, and full around the ears), all give her appearance Viennese authenticity.

She has cultivated the Viennese art of living well and fully to a high degree. There is nothing effete or jaded about her. Her enthusiasms are many, and always fresh and alive. Her life is crowded with activity and diversion. Music, of course, is the major sphere of her activity. But Lehmann would not be a true Viennese in temperament if music, and music alone, dominated her life. She loves to read good literature—and reads it voraciously. Better still she loves to write it. Writing to her is no mere hobby, but an essential artistic expression. At times, she finds the urge to put pen to paper almost as strong as that to sing. Creative writing, in her life, holds a place only second to that of music. She has published many poems and articles in leading magazines, and a charming novel entitled *Eternal Flight*. Her autobiography, *Midway in My Song*, is suffused with the magnetism and warmth of her personality. Other books are always in the process of composition.

But Lehmann's life is so well organized that she has time not only for two exacting arts, but for lighter diversions as well—such as horseback riding and swimming, both of which she does with professional expertness. Nor did her many activities prevent her from partaking in the homely simplicity of a quiet evening with her husband, while he was alive, which afforded her one of the greatest shares of personal delight.

Her essential simplicity of character is the simplicity which has made the Viennese the most lovable people in the world. She makes no attempt to envelope herself in a self-assured glamour, postures or affectations are altogether alien to her nature. Viennese, too, is her hospitality, known to everyone who has had contact with her. In the presence of her guests Lehmann exudes an atmosphere of conviviality and warmth of feeling which makes them feel always comfortable and at ease. Viennese is her genius in endowing any place in which she lives (even a hotel room) with the unique charm of her personality. Unfortunately, her extensive travels throughout the world make it impossible for Lehmann —essentially a domestic soul—to enjoy very much of home life. She has several residences, some of them spacious, but no *home* in the strictest meaning of the word. However, Lehmann has an extraordinary capacity for permeating even a transitory residence with character.

There is an all-embracing cordiality in the Lehmann living room, an atmosphere of comfort and repose. No sooner does she unpack in a new setting—and every few days there is a new setting for Lehmann!—and hang her favorite portraits on the walls ("Home," she will tell you, "is where I hang my pictures"), than suddenly, by magic, the place acquires something of the personality of a permanent abode.

Too many writers, in describing Lehmann's personal life, have overdrawn their characterizations almost to a point of caricature. Lehmann is *not*, as some writers have suggested, a typical Viennese *Hausfrau;* she has neither the temperament nor the interest to concern herself with the management of a home. She is utterly incapable of Viennese parsimoniousness, a trait which some writers have unjustly attributed to her. As a matter of fact, one of her great passions is the extravagant presentation of gifts to friends. She never comes to a city without being amply supplied with tokens for each and every one of her circle. She has a flair for buying expensive knick-knacks that are utterly useless.

3

A small town near Hamburg, Germany—Perleberg, not far from the North Sea—was the birthplace of Lotte

Lehmann. Her childhood was not unusual. Memories of her early years today bring up to Lehmann's mind charming images: red plush furniture in a rather warm and comfortable house; her mother, who was all softness and solicitude; and her father, a small-town official, practical and strong-minded, who combined a love for his daughter with an insistence on strong discipline.

Herr Lehmann—at peace with the world because, being a government official, he would be provided for by a government pension when he was ready to retire —was determined, almost from Lotte's birth, that she should know a similar blessing. He was thinking particularly of a career as schoolteacher for his daughter. From Lotte's early childhood his energy and industry were directed into preparing her for the chosen field. He gave her the benefits of a well-rounded education—music, languages, drawing, the elements of science. When, many years later, Lotte Lehmann became an opera singer, Herr Lehmann's lament was that the glory of an artist, sweet though it was, was only ephemeral; only a government pension brought stability. Not until Lotte Lehmann became a permanent member of the Vienna Opera did her father know peace of mind. For as a member of the Vienna State Opera she was entitled to a government pension.

When Lotte was in her early 'teens, her family moved

to Berlin where the attempt to make her a schoolteacher was intensified. She was enrolled in a local high school where she proved to be a bright but uninterested pupil. She was much more preoccupied with the writing of poetry than in the sciences—one poem she actually sold to an editor for two dollars. And she indulged in schoolgirl flirtations and puppy-love more assiduously than in her school exercises.

As a girl, Lotte had a small and pleasant voice, with which she often entertained her close friends in performances of songs. It was through the influence of a neighbor that she was given admittance into the Royal Academy of Music in Berlin. Music now absorbed her interest and enthusiasms as nothing had succeeded in doing until now, not even the writing of poetry. She was inflamed by a personal ambition for the first time in her life. She would be a concert artist.

While still a music student, Lotte Lehmann experienced her first serious love affair. He was a broad-chested, blond-haired handsome young man named Willy. There was the usual whispering of soft words, and holding of hands, the exchange of promises. Soon there was even talk of marriage, and elaborate plans for the future. Then the question of Lotte's singing arose. Willy was determined that Lotte should surrender every thought of a career and devote herself entirely to home, husband and children. In his forceful Teutonic manner, Willy placed the choice squarely in Lotte's hands: she was to select either a singing career or marriage. Lotte Lehmann did not hesitate in making her choice.

In looking back upon her first years as a music student Lotte Lehmann today recognizes what a profound debt she owes to her older brother, Fritz, now teacher of a dramatic class. His meager purse, his mature counsel, his encouragement were always at hand when Lotte needed them—and during those early years Lotte needed all three desperately. That her way was made so much smoother was largely the result of his conscientious devotion; and that devotion she has never forgotten.

Following her studies at the Royal Academy of Music, Lotte Lehmann became a private pupil of Mathilde Mallinger, a well-known Wagnerian singer. To Mallinger belongs the distinction of being the first to recognize Lehmann's great talent, and to guess that, with proper preparation, a magnificent career awaited her. She gave her protégé an intensive training.

Equipped with this training, which had transformed Lehmann from a blundering student into an integrated musician, she applied for a small position as singer at the Hamburg Opera House. She was given a three-year contract at a salary of two hundred marks a month (fifty dollars). Shortly after joining the opera house, she made her début as Freia in Wagner's *Rheingold*.

Her début passed without any favorable notice. Some critics were even acidulously disparaging. "A Fraulein Lehmann sang and played the part of Freia with touching awkwardness," commented the *Hamburger Fremdenblatt*. "As to the vocal qualities of the young lady, whose throat seemed constricted by excessive nervousness, we can as yet say nothing." But Lehmann was not discouraged. For a long time, she continued to perform small parts.

But—though it seemed that no one was aware of her existence—her work did not pass entirely unnoticed. The musical director of the Hamburg Opera was the young but already well-known conductor, Otto Klemperer. Klemperer had silently watched Lehmann's work and had been impressed by it. Then, when the sudden illness of the Wagnerian soprano, Fleischer-Edel, demanded an immediate substitute, he approached Lehmann and asked her if she would care to try the rôle of Elsa in *Lohengrin*.

I shall permit Lotte Lehmann herself to describe an event which was unquestionably the turning point in her career.

"Would I care to try the rôle of Elsa? Did Herr

Klemperer have to ask me *that?* I had already studied the part by myself and I felt I knew every note of it. I came to the first rehearsal, therefore, somewhat sure of myself and my ground, and as proud as a peacock. But if I deluded myself into believing that I knew the rôle thoroughly, I was soon to see the error of my delusion. Klemperer sat at the piano like some wild demon, throwing his long hands, like tiger's paws, upon the keys, guiding me by the sheer force of his fanatic will. For the first time in my life I felt all constraining shyness fall from me completely. The rôle suddenly became the flame of my personal experience. I felt I was transfigured. I should have liked to sing this way forever, without interruption. But suddenly, a crash awakened me from my dreams. The voice of Klemperer rudely tore me from my raptures. 'You have no idea of the part,' he growled. 'You must try again, and then again, and work much more carefully.' With each lapse of memory, he would become increasingly angry and call to me, 'What is the matter *now?* I suppose Elsa's crown has turned your head!' But I was always blessed with stubbornness, and I continued working on the rôle with indefatigable ardor.

"The evening of the performance I did not see the audience; I did not even see the face of the director. I forgot everything—where I was, what the evening meant to me. I was Elsa, the Elsa that was first revealed to me by Klemperer, the Elsa that I now fully understood for the first time. Tears came to my eyes as the chorus sang *Heil dir Elsa von Brabant*. And *Heil dir* my whole heart sings to the day of days which was the real beginning of my life."

4

Having been discovered by Klemperer and assigned major rôles not only in German but also in French and Italian operas, it was not long before Lehmann became one of the principal sopranos of the Hamburg Opera. Greater experience brought her the self-assurance she needed. To each of her rôles she now brought the illumination of her personality—having acquired the self-confidence to give it full revelation—and an increasing richness of voice. The audiences began to speak of her performances in rapturous tones.

One evening, she was singing the rôle of Micaela in *Carmen*. In the audience was the director of the Vienna Court Opera who had come to Hamburg to engage its leading tenor for several guest performances in his own opera house. After the performance of *Carmen* he rushed backstage. Completely forgetting the tenor he had come to engage, he insisted he must procure Lehmann for Vienna.

Thus it was that Lehmann was brought to the city

where she achieved her first great triumphs, the city which was to become her home for so many years, the city which had known and adored another Lehmann, the great Lilli (who is not related to Lotte) and which was soon to transfer that adoration to the younger woman. In Vienna were unfolded the operatic characterizations which were to spread Lehmann's reputation to the four corners of the world—Sieglinde in *Die Walküre*, the Marschallin in the *Rosenkavalier*, Leonore in *Fidelio*. In Vienna she first emerged as a singer of dramatic songs in a series of recitals which soon proved to be the great artistic event of the year. It was at a rehearsal in Vienna that Richard Strauss first heard her sing, and was so moved by her performance that he immediately designated her for the rôle of the Young Composer in his opera *Ariadne auf Naxos*. A few years later the master was to compose his opera *Arabella* expressly for Lotte Lehmann.

As a mark of its appreciation for the great artist in its midst, Vienna awarded Lehmann the highest decoration which the government could bestow on an artist, and with it the title of *Kammersängerin* and honorary member.

A few years later, still another government was to recognize Lehmann's genius officially—France. It appointed her Officer of the Legion of Honor, the only woman artist of a foreign country ever to receive that award.

It was in Vienna, too, that Lotte Lehmann met Otto Krause, a dashing cavalier—formerly an officer in the Austrian army, and an extraordinary horseback rider—who might very easily have stepped from the pages of a Schnitzler novel. Krause heard Lehmann sing at the Opera one evening. He felt as if a spell had come over him. From that time on, he was always in the opera house on the evenings that Lehmann appeared, occupying the same seat.

They met at a party. That was the beginning of a romance which was climaxed with their marriage in 1926. His death in January, 1939, was a great blow to Lehmann.

Engagements in the leading opera houses in Europe followed her triumphant successes in Vienna. Wherever Lehmann performed she was royally received. Perhaps her greatest personal victory came in Paris in 1927. For the first time since the World War, a German opera was to be introduced at the Paris Opéra—Beethoven's *Fidelio*, in honor of the centenary celebration of the composer's birth. Lotte Lehmann was invited to sing the rôle of Leonore. *Fidelio* had been included in the repertory with no little misgiving. The French were still anti-German, and there was no telling how they would react to their first German opera since 1914. It was Lehmann's art, even more than Beethoven's, that conquered the prejudice and hatred of an audience. An audience that greeted the opening passages of the opera with apathy was swept to enthusiasm by Lehmann's singing, until it rose to cheer her at the end of the opera. As one lady is reported to have whispered to her neighbor: "I know I should hate her, for she is German. But how can one possibly hate a person with such a heavenly voice?"

Following successful performances at the Salzburg festival, of which she was to become one of the major cornerstones for the next few years, Lehmann came to America and made her début at the Chicago Opera Company on October 28, 1930. These successful appearances in Chicago were merely the forerunners of performances throughout the country—both in opera and in recitals of *Lieder*—in which her prestige mounted. Finally, on January 11, 1934, she made her Metropolitan Opera House début as Sieglinde in *Die Walküre*.

"Never before," reported one critic, "in the history of the Metropolitan Opera House has there been such a success. Wagnerian audiences do not enthuse to a very great extent, but the instant the curtain fell, the applause rang out spontaneously. Then when Lotte Lehmann came before the footlights, it rose in volume, and as her confrères left her alone—something rare in the first curtain call—the whole audience broke into cheering which lasted a full ten minutes."

Lotte Lehmann's career in America, as one of its best loved singers of opera and song, was now fully launched.

Early in 1938, Lotte Lehmann renounced her homeland and announced that she would become a citizen of the United States. What pain this permanent separation from her beloved Vienna has brought her, only her most intimate friends know. As Lehmann herself has written in the preface of her engaging autobiography: "My blood is German and my whole being is rooted in the German soil. But my conception of art is different from that of my country. . . . I no longer understand the land of my birth."

And, just as in 1933 Lehmann renounced her native country, Germany, so in 1938 she broke her still stronger ties with her adopted homeland, Austria. She is now an American; the United States is her new homeland.

Artur Schnabel

IX: SCHNABEL

CHAPTER NINE

ARTUR SCHNABEL

UPON four different occasions, Artur Schnabel has given a comprehensive cycle of concerts devoted to the thirty-two piano sonatas of Beethoven—twice in Berlin, once in London, and once in New York. He has recorded all the Beethoven piano sonatas on phonograph records, and has edited and annotated a new publication of these sonatas. He has also recorded all the five piano concertos of the master, as well as the *Diabelli Variations*. Finally, Beethoven's music has almost inevitably appeared on his programs during the span of his career. Schnabel, therefore, has handsomely deserved the designation often given him by critics—that of "Beethoven's high-priest."

Schnabel realizes that it is a shortcoming for any interpreter to devote himself so completely to the music of any one composer. "Make no mistake," he once said not without a slight touch of irony. "It is my limitation that I play so much Beethoven. But I am completely happy in my one-sidedness."

But Schnabel need make no elaborate apologies for his artistic devotion to Beethoven. For one thing, the piano music of Beethoven—much more, I believe, than the piano works of any other one composer, not excluding Johann Sebastian Bach—embraces so many different styles, so many diverse messages, such a variety of mood and atmosphere that a great interpreter of these sonatas must have the plasticity of approach and technique which are required for the interpretation of music by many different composers. From the classicism of the Opus 2 to the symphonic dynamics of Opus 111 is a mighty expanse, which no interpreter need be ashamed of claiming as his entire world.

Besides, Schnabel's artistic career has not been quite so one-sided as some have claimed. True, a Schnabel program is usually more confining than the programs of other pianists. He is sparing with Chopin, Liszt, Debussy—if he plays these composers at all. And the music of modern composers, particularly during the past twenty years, has not been featured by him. Schnabel is no enemy of modern music. As a matter of fact, two of the foremost living modernists, Paul Hindemith and Arnold Schönberg, are his personal friends. And—curious fact to record!—in his own compositions, Schnabel is brazenly audacious in his use of harmonic combinations. But, being a severely honest artist, Schnabel refuses to play any music which does not move him profoundly. "An artist," he has said, "should and does choose to play only that music of which he is particularly fond. And the field of what he likes should be wide enough."

As a matter of fact, Schnabel's own field of preferences *is* wide enough. He has played Mozart often—and beautifully. For Bach's music he has a decided preference, and he gives it all the breadth of design and proportion it requires. For a long time he was considered by many in Europe one of the greatest living interpreters of the piano music of Johannes Brahms. His Schubert (above all) has warmth, tenderness, an exquisite delicacy; many critics put it even above his Beethoven. When he plays Schumann, he discloses a profound insight into the pianistic style and musical content of the great Romanticist. With these composers, he feels, his artistic life is complete. "No matter how long my life is, it will be too short to get through with Bach, Mozart, Beethoven, Schubert, Schumann and Brahms. There is a necessity in me to play these composers."

Schnabel has, at times, been even more frequently criticized for what some choose to call his "austere intellectualism" as a pianist—and with even less justification. He is intellectual, if by that word we imply the ability to analyze a musical work profoundly, and in a performance to reveal the fruits of such painstaking analysis. He is an intellectual, too, if that word is to be applied loosely to musicians who adhere meticulously to the printed wish of the composer. But there is nothing cut-and-dried about Schnabel's performances. They are by no means over-cerebralized, or lacking in emotion. Schnabel is not the one to yield to emotional excess, to make music—so to speak—the refuse place for his emotions. But his playing is always full of feeling, and is always moving. One has merely to recall his playing of the *Hammerklavier Sonata* of Beethoven in which the bizarre series of trills in the last movement, for example, the noble resignation of the slow movement, the iron-fisted defiance of the opening chords, receive at his hands a performance blending poignancy and power. One has merely to recall the youthfulness with which he endows the Schubert B-flat major (posthumous) Sonata, or the emotional storms that sweep through his rendition of the Brahms B-flat major Concerto.

Schnabel, the pedant—the emotionally sterile intellectual? Absurd. He himself has often spoken eloquently on behalf of a greater emotional approach to music. "I assure you," he has said in an interview—a message which he has frequently repeated in more than one form, "that it is only when I forget my craftsmanship that I begin to enjoy music. . . . If you want to learn all you can about music, that is splendid. But if you think that by learning you can make yourself love music, you are very much mistaken. . . . You do not have to be a botanist to enjoy flowers growing in a meadow. All this emphasis on learning and understanding music! Music should not be learned and understood, half so much as it should be loved and enjoyed. One can understand it through love."

But why do we need his words, when his own playing has said this so unmistakably?

2

Though from certain quarters Schnabel may receive criticism which is largely unjustified, his importance as an interpreter is rarely questioned. That he is one of the great pianists of our time, and one of the greatest living interpreters of Beethoven is generally conceded. Yet his victory in this country was not an immediate one. Because his art was unsensational, and his personality without magnetism, it was many years before he received recognition here.

He came to America for the first time in 1922. Yet, though he played then quite as magnificently as he does today, he was received here coldly and apathetically. One reason perhaps was the fact that, though he enjoyed at the time a solid reputation in Europe, his career offered little material for dramatization, little material with which to arouse the country and inflame the imagination of a virtuoso-crazy public.

He was born in Lipnik, Austria, on April 17, 1882, and began the study of music at an early age. When he was seven, he was the pupil of Hans Schmitt. Schnabel's progress was so rapid that when he was eight years old he made several successful concert appearances. It was decided to give him the best instruction in Vienna. In 1891, he became a pupil of the great Leschetizky, the teacher of Ignace Jan Paderewski; his fellow pupils at the time included Ossip Gabrilowitsch and Mark Hambourg. In Leschetizky's famous home on the Carl Ludwigstrasse, Schnabel breathed in a musical atmosphere. The most famous musicians of Vienna came to Leschetizky's home to hear his pupils play, among them Johannes Brahms, Ignaz Brüll, Karl Goldmark, and the visiting Anton Rubinstein. Brahms heard Schnabel play one day, accosted him, and exclaimed: "How in the name of heaven can you play all this so correctly?"

Schnabel remained Leschetizky's pupil for six years. Then his concert life began. What followed was the slow and inevitable growth of an artist, but the biographical material is not dramatic. He gave sonata recitals with Carl Flesch, the violinist, joint recitals with his wife, Therese Behr, an extraordinary *Lieder* singer, and performed in trios. Always was his fine musicianship subject to praise. He gave piano recitals in Berlin. His reputation grew rapidly, and concert tours followed throughout Europe. His performances of Beethoven and Brahms were acclaimed everywhere. He appeared as soloist with the leading European orchestras, and under the batons of the foremost conductors, in concertos of Mozart, Beethoven and Brahms. Following the World War, he was generally recognized as one of the foremost of European pianists. In 1919 he was given the Honorary Professor degree by the Prussian State.

If his background was unspectacular to New York music audiences of 1922, what then could one say about his personality? When he stepped on the stage he resembled more the successful business man than the great artist. No lithe or supple lines of the body, no romantic shock of hair, no poetic expression. He was short and stockily built. His head, large and well formed, was covered with closely cropped and bristling hair. A moustache, thick as a brush, accentuated the full roundness of his face. He was, most assuredly, an unromantic figure to the eye. Even his manners at the piano were hardly calculated to arouse infatuation. He played without flourishes, or extravagant movements of the body. He played with despatch—played like a man who knows his business and can attend to it efficiently.

MEN AND WOMEN WHO MAKE MUSIC

The New York music audiences of 1922, which liked to apotheosize its concert artists, did not take to him. Schnabel toured the country, and again the following year—then, disappointed, resumed his concert career in Europe (where he was being appreciated more and more each year) and devoted himself industriously to teaching the piano. For many years he was the leader of a master class at the Prussian State Academy of Music.

It was seven years before he returned to America, where he had experienced perhaps the greatest failure of his career. But, at the insistence of his personal friends and pupils, he returned—a little more than a decade after his first visit. He found that the musical life in America had changed radically. "America seems to have reached maturity," he said. "It has left slowly the pioneering stage and mass production era. New artistic and spiritual things may be enjoyed more and more." The emphasis now was placed not on the virtuoso but on his playing; the American public had outgrown its fad for romantic concert artists. What it demanded now was great performances, and, moreover, great music. Into such a scheme of things Schnabel could fit most harmoniously.

His success in America was soon established. This was proved eloquently in 1935 when he gave his monumental cycle of the Beethoven piano sonatas at Carnegie Hall. His managers at first attempted to discourage him from such an undertaking, saying that the response to such a Gargantuan venture could not be adequate. But Schnabel had faith that New York was ripe for the adventure. And his faith was justified. Eighteen thousand people attended the seven concerts of Beethoven's sonatas, paying in excess of $23,000—an unheard of achievement for a series of piano recitals.

3

Mention should be made of the fact that Artur Schnabel is one of the great piano teachers of our time—a worthy successor to his own master, Leschetizky. Schnabel's beautiful home on Lake Como, in Italy, has become almost as famous as the Carl Ludwigstrasse house of Leschetizky. That home is the goal of ever so many young piano students, upon the completion of their studies, just as the Leschetizky studio was the aspiration of piano pupils several decades ago. Many famous pianists have attained maturity under Schnabel's tuition.

Each summer at Lake Como there gather outstanding young pianists eager to bring their study to consummation, and to prepare for concert appearances under Schnabel's guidance. There are no private lessons. Each pupil comes with his own repertoire, but plays not only before the teacher but before the other students as well.

An engaging informality and warmth of feeling exist between teacher and pupils. The class gathers in a studio where for a short while preceding the lesson pupils and teacher smoke, chat, exchange stories. But once work begins the air becomes tense with seriousness of purpose. What follows is a gruelling period of work for both teacher and pupils. Schnabel has an enormous capacity for work, and a driving force which necessitates hard work on the part of those who study under him.

One pupil is told to perform a composition he has prepared. Schnabel listens attentively to the performance and then makes some generalized comments about the interpretation as a whole. Seating himself at a second piano, Schnabel then passes from the general to the specific. There follows a minute and painstaking dissection of every detail of the pupil's playing—his phrasing, nuance, touch, tone, pedal-work, etc. Also, bar by bar, the musical work is subjected to analysis. Sometimes several hours are required for one musical work, but Schnabel does not stop until he has said his final words, and until he is confident that the student has absorbed his lessons. Once he is sure of this, he will have no further comment to make, and will refuse to have a pupil perform the composition again.

Schnabel teaches three periods three times a week. The first period begins at a specific hour—usually at eight in the morning—but ends, no one can tell when. A lesson is not over until Schnabel is through, and Schnabel is not through until he has made clear every point he wishes to emphasize about a given work. Often the students feel, at the end, limp with exhaustion. But they also feel that they have been given a profound understanding of a musical work, and a penetrating dissection of the performance it received.

By the time a summer of study comes to an end, each student has had the opportunity of hearing almost a hundred masterpieces of piano literature analyzed by Schnabel. Thus equipped, the student is ready for concert work. "We have all learned some things from each other's virtues and mistakes," Schnabel has said. "One thing I try to impress on my students above everything else—and that is that life is fundamentally serious, and so is study and a career. But I also warn them not to be too earnest about being serious."

X: ORMANDY

Eugene Ormandy

CHAPTER TEN

EUGENE ORMANDY

WHEN Eugene Ormandy accepted the post of permanent conductor of the Philadelphia Symphony Orchestra, his friends told him that he was undertaking an
impossible assignment. To direct one of the great orchestras in America with only limited experience was in itself a man-sized job. But Ormandy was facing an even
greater problem. He had to replace the glamorous and
incomparable Stokowski who, during his twenty years of
conducting the Philadelphia Orchestra, had become the
autocrat of the Philadelphia and New York symphony
hall. In the eyes of his audiences, Stokowski had been
"the one-and-only." He was believed to be irreplacable.
Anybody trying to fill his shoes, they said, was committing nothing less than artistic suicide. Some went so far
as to say that when Stokowski went, there was nothing for
the Philadelphia Orchestra to do but to shut up shop;
the audiences simply would not come to hear any other
conductor.

But Ormandy has achieved what some music lovers
choose to call a miracle. Despite his formerly limited

conductorial background, his concerts have had authority and great musical appeal. Few first-ranking conductors from European capitals could have maintained a higher artistic level for the Philadelphia concerts than Ormandy. But Ormandy has accomplished even more than this. He has replaced Stokowski—the "incomparable Stokowski"—in the admiration of his public. No, they have not forgotten Stokowski at the Philadelphia concerts. The few times he has come back to give a guest performance with his orchestra he has been given a great welcome. But Ormandy, almost from his first concerts, completely sold himself to his audiences.

Ormandy was no stranger to Philadelphia. The dawn of his conductorial career broke in Philadelphia with a few impressive guest appearances. And that city knew well that, though Ormandy did not come to his new post with a luminous European reputation trailing him, he came with a far more potent equipment. He came with a formidable talent, with profound musicianship, with tact and instinct, with personal appeal and magnetism. It was not long, therefore, before the Philadelphia audiences became Ormandy "fans," as they had been Stokowski "fans" a few years previously.

Just how far Ormandy has gone in replacing his lustrous predecessor became apparent a short time ago when the announcement came that he had been given the office of "music director" of the Philadelphia Orchestra. The office of "music director" is quite apart from that of conductor. It was created some years back to give Stokowski full dictatorial powers. In passing on so high an office, established expressly for Stokowski, to young Ormandy, the board of directors of the Philadelphia Orchestra has given him its most convincing vote of confidence.

2

When one looks back upon the years of Ormandy's direction in Philadelphia, one realizes that a part of his success at least has been bought with some of the coin used by Stokowski. The similarity betwen Stokowski and Ormandy is striking even after one has penetrated beyond superficial exteriors. Like Stokowski, Ormandy is blond, graceful; he cuts a fine figure on the conductor's stand. Like Stokowski, Ormandy is American-made, acquiring his reputation in a phenomenally short time; Stokowski rose to fame in three years in Cincinnati, and an almost similar length of time brought Ormandy from comparative obscurity to nationwide attention in Minneapolis. Like Stokowski, Ormandy conducts without a score in front of him, and for one season has even directed without a baton—the latter, one of Stokowski's most recognizable trade-marks. Stokowski's concerts were famous for his own orchestral transcriptions of Bach's music. Orchestral transcriptions of Bach still predominate on Philadelphia programs, although the transcriptions are now the work of Lucien Caillet, a member of the orchestra, instead of the conductor. Like Stokowski, Ormandy has the intuitive faculty of making his orchestra *sound;* even when his interpretations are second-rate, his orchestra plays with beautiful tone and rich sonority to delight the ear. Finally, like Stokowski, Ormandy keeps his concerts alive by injecting into them the vitality of experiment and novelty. He plays the classical masterpieces, of course, but he is an apostle of modern music as well. Ormandy has learned an all-important lesson from his predecessor: a smug audience soon becomes a bored one.

But when you look back critically on Ormandy's work you soon realize that Ormandy is not merely a photostatic copy of his forerunner. He is temperamentally incapable of imitating the Barnum stunts which—year in, year out—brought Stokowski's name on the front pages. Ormandy is a serious young man who devotes himself to his art with integrity and devotion. He is utterly unable to make music his trapeze for circus-tricks. You will not find Ormandy making pretty and carefully rehearsed speeches to ladies who rattle their programs, or rehearsing his orchestra astride a dummy horse, or running off to Capri with the first lady of Hollywood. Ormandy takes his music-making too earnestly to find time for such picturesque exploits. Studying the scores that come to his desk is a full day's occupation for him. Where the reading of manuscripts is concerned, Ormandy is conscientiousness itself. And whipping his orchestra into shape for every concert is an all-exhausting occupation. Stokowski before him was never such a stickler for detail as he is. He has almost Toscanini's passionate devotion for thoroughness, for the perfection of every phrase and line. What he lacks in experience, he more than makes up with sincerity and artistic devotion. He is a hard worker; and he is a good conductor because he is capable of making his men hard workers.

3

He achieved the impossible when he so completely replaced Stokowski. But doing the impossible has by no means been an infrequent feat for Ormandy. His career, as a matter of fact, has been marked by the assumption of formidable assignments which he has quietly and efficiently fulfilled with unpredictable success. The first of these took place about ten years ago, when Ormandy was concertmaster in the orchestra of the Capitol Theatre. At that time, David Mendoza, the conductor of the orchestra, was scheduled to conduct three movements of Tschaikovsky's Fourth Symphony. Sudden illness made his appearance impossible. No substitute was available at the moment, so Roxy, the manager—upon the advice of some violinists in the orchestra—asked Ormandy to try his hand with the baton. Ormandy heeded the call, even though he had never before conducted an orchestra. Not only did he direct the music with authority and despatch, but—to the bewilderment of his fellow-musicians—he conducted the music from memory. After that, Ormandy was added to the staff of the Capitol Theatre conductors.

Ormandy's second imposing assignment came in 1931. By this time, he had achieved a reputation for his radio work as conductor on the Columbia Broadcasting System, and for his guest appearances as conductor of the Philadelphia Orchestra and the Stadium Concerts in New York. In 1931, Toscanini was scheduled to conduct several performances with the Philadelphia Orchestra. A sudden attack of neuritis forced Toscanini to postpone his appearance. A long list of possible substitutes was depleted before the distraught managers came upon the name of Ormandy. His friends warned him against substituting for Toscanini, told him that many of the other conductors that had been approached had turned down the offer because they refused to invite the inevitable comparison with the greatest conductor of the age. But

Ormandy was deaf to advice. He was so successful that, a few days later, he received a call from Minneapolis to become first, guest, then, permanent conductor of its orchestra.

It was during this five-year period as conductor of the Minneapolis Orchestra that Ormandy established a reputation as a conductor of great talent. From the badly balanced orchestra capable only of inert and lackadaisical performances that had been the Minneapolis under Henri Verbrugghen, it amplified its sonority, expanded its technical resources and enriched its tone so that, in two years, it seems to be an entirely different organization. He also courageously undertook a vast repertoire that included not merely the classics but the bulk of the most representative modern music from Mahler and Bruckner to Schönberg and Kodály. Under him the Minneapolis Orchestra became one of the major orchestral institutions in the country.

When Stokowski resigned as permanent conductor in Philadelphia to assume other duties in Hollywood, the enviable position was offered—not to a famous European leader—but to the young director of Minneapolis. In Philadelphia Ormandy grew as an artist. There were now few who did not consider him the foremost of the younger conductors in America.

4

Ormandy's career, therefore, has been rich with material which no doubt will some day be fashioned by idolatrous audiences into legends. But the material extends back much farther than his early years in America.

Born in Budapest on November 18, 1899, Ormandy revealed a phenomenal gift for music almost in his cradle. When he was one and a half years old, he could name any one of fifty musical works after hearing only the first few bars on a music box. At three, he began the study of the violin, and at once revealed an ear for perfect pitch and an infallible musical instinct. Leading musicians in Budapest tested him endlessly, played the most difficult harmonic combinations on the piano and asked the boy—who was blindfolded—to name the various notes. To Eugene, this was much easier than skipping rope.

He was five years old when he was enrolled in the Budapest Academy of Music, the youngest pupil ever admitted to that institution. At seven he made his début as a violinist. It is said that when he made his first appearance, his teacher asked him to play from notes as a safeguard against nervousness. But self-assured, little Eugene felt that no concessions need be made to his age. He insisted on playing from memory and did so faultlessly.

Ormandy continued to be a precocious student. After a period of study under the great Hungarian violinist, Jenö Hubay, he received a master's degree from the Conservatory. He was only fourteen then—six years younger than other recipients of the degree. When he was nineteen, he was appointed full "professor of music" at the Conservatory. His colleagues were middle-aged men, some of them with beards.

Some moderately successful concert tours followed. An impresario then approached Ormandy, bringing him wondrous tales of the fabulous success enjoyed by the Jaschas, Toschas and Mischas of the violin in New York. He promised Ormandy a tour that would span the country and bring him fame and fortune.

In 1920, Ormandy came to America, his hopes soaring. But he was soon enough deflated. The manager, he learned, had been day-dreaming. He had neither the connections nor the funds with which to launch a concert tour for Ormandy.

Stranded, Ormandy accepted the first job that came to him. He became a violinist of the Capitol Theatre orchestra. Geographically, the Capitol Theatre is only a few streets from Carnegie Hall. As far as Ormandy was concerned they were in different worlds, the distance between which—he now felt—he could never hope to span.

When he did span the distance, it was not as a concert violinist but as a conductor of symphony orchestras.

5

Eugene Ormandy is one of the youngest conductors in the world to hold a symphony post of first importance. He appears even younger than his age. He is blond-haired, of medium height, well built. His face has an expression of almost boyish ingenuousness. Away from the concert hall, he is admired for his sincerity, soft-spoken modesty, and seriousness of purpose.

Whatever he does, he does with intensity—whether it is conducting music, playing ping-pong or tennis. It might be mentioned that Ormandy is one of the top-ranking ping-pong players in the country, and that he was a tennis champion in amateur competitions in Austria a few years back. He is also a good student. After graduating from the University of Budapest, he took elective courses in psychology with the expectation of receiving a doctorate degree. He passed his final examinations, but did not get his degree because he neglected to write his thesis. A few years ago Ormandy received an honorary doctorate from Hamlin University, and in 1937, another one from the University of Pennsylvania.

Ormandy possesses one other talent which may or may

not be illuminating in explaining his conductorial success. As a student of psychology, Ormandy disclosed amazing hypnotic powers, actually giving several successful amateur seances in the presence of distinguished Budapest psychologists. He was finally compelled to give up hypnotism because he found that it proved harmful to his nervous system.

But any number of orchestra men, who have played under him, must wonder if he has really given up the practice completely.

XI: CASALS

CHAPTER ELEVEN

PABLO CASALS

WHEN, in the summer of 1936, Civil War broke out in Spain, friends of Pablo Casals urged him to leave Barcelona and carry on his art in quieter and more gratifying surroundings. To such entreaties, Casals made an answer characteristic of him. In these difficult hours, he said, the Spanish people needed music more than ever before. It was unthinkable for him to desert his people—now that they could turn to art to succor them and give them spiritual strength.

If he would leave for other European capitals, it would be for one reason alone. He would concertize extensively to raise money for Spain, to help his country materially as well as spiritually in its war against Fascist invasion.

And so, with his native Spain torn and bleeding, Casals summoned his art to help his people. He concertized extensively in France and England so that the money he earned might be translated into sadly needed food, clothing and supplies. Between tours he returned to Barcelona to continue conducting his famous concerts of symphonic music, and playing his violoncello. The city might be paralyzed by war. Bombs from Italian planes might drop perilously near the concert hall. Scarcity of food might raise the gruesome specter of starvation. The hospitals might be filled with the crippled and the dying, many of them non-combatants, innocent victims of foreign air attacks. But music in Spain went on to capacity audiences, because their director felt that Spain needed a spiritual haven from madness.

Casals' career as an artist has been marked by other similar gestures of self-denial and nobility. His greatness as a human being is comparable only to his stature as an artist. Those who know him well—and I have spoken to some of his most intimate friends—speak of his ascetic simplicity, his directness, his scrupulous honesty, and above all else, the rich vein of nobility in him.

Long before 1936—in happier days for Spain—he showed his allegiance to his country and his devotion to his people. The foundation of his world-famous Orquestra Pau Casals is a significant example.

Barcelona had had symphony orchestras before, but always their life span was brief. It was said that Catalonians were too poor to support a permanent symphony orchestra. More important still, it was said that they were too unmusical to appreciate one.

Casals lamented the fact that in Barcelona there was

194

Pablo Casals

absent so important a cultural influence as a permanent orchestra. He made contact with important musicians, patrons, government officials, and urged the formation of a good symphonic organization on a permanent basis. But wherever he went he met with pessimism. It was a hopeless dream, he was told. Catalonians simply did not interest themselves in great music. For their tastes, café-house orchestras were ample.

But Casals did not admit defeat. He had money, and his violoncello brought him a substantial income. He had important artistic connections. He decided that, on his own responsibility, he would organize a permanent symphony orchestra in Barcelona. He combed the city for the best musicians available, guaranteed them their salaries from his own pocketbook, and set to work.

The difficulties which then faced Casals were heartbreaking, and would have broken a spirit less defiant than his. Political differences among the musicians almost disrupted the newborn organization. Only the infinite tact of the conductor smoothed over such differences of opinion. Musical problems were even more formidable. Some of the musicians had never played in an orchestra. To coordinate their work, to organize them into a unified body—in some cases even to teach them the essential technique—required herculean work on the part of Casals, particularly since from the very first he insisted upon addressing himself only to the greatest music. He worked so slavishly and with such undivided concentration that, at one time, he broke down physically and was forced to discontinue his efforts for a while.

Finally, the first concert took place, on October 13, 1920, at the Music Auditorium of the Catalan Palace. The response to the new orchestra, at first, was cool. But Casals had faith in his mission. He continued defraying all the expenses. He continued his fastidious preparation for each concert. Then, slowly, subscriptions began to increase; the hall became more and more crowded. At last, there were capacity audiences. Casals' orchestra had achieved permanency.

Having achieved what so many had said was impossible—the establishment of a great orchestra in Barcelona—Casals was not satisfied. He was soon fired with another, and still greater mission. He wanted great music to reach not only people who could pay the price, but also the lowest-paid workmen of Barcelona, to whom the price of admission to concerts was prohibitive. Early in his life, Casals read Karl Marx passionately. After that, his humanitarian interest for the under-dog of society never deserted him. Now he wished to translate theory into practice. He wished to do something tangible and important for the worker. He wanted to bring him great music, the greatest music, at prices he could afford to pay.

Once again, Casals was faced with staggering difficulties (not the least of which was the skepticism of the
workers themselves, who were suspicious of anyone
bringing them something for nothing). Once again he
encountered argument and discouragement which would
have disheartened so many others. But once again he
triumphed over difficulties through the sheer force of his
will. He evolved a musical organization for workers
which, for a few cents, entitled them to participation in a
variety of musical activities, including attendance at six
Sunday morning concerts of Casals' orchestra. For these
concerts, Casals maintained a rigorously high artistic
standard, and was often inspired by the magnificent reception his music received from the workers.

2

About Casals' conducting, Mr. Fox-Strangways, distinguished critic of the London *Observer*, has written:
"He plays as if he held a responsible trust, determined
that at all costs the purity of the faith shall not suffer
at his hands. He refrains from anything histrionic or
ephemeral; he wants the truth of it. So the tempi of
Beethoven's Seventh Symphony were what excitable
people call 'dry.' They do not realize how much they
have destroyed Beethoven and Brahms for us by their

fussy sentimentality, and that the only way to get these back is to mean every word of them, as he does. . . . In whatever he does, he seems to aim at some invisible and unattainable ideal, and if some part of that is reached immediately to set the standard higher."

However, it is as a violoncellist, rather than as a conductor, that Pablo Casals is for many of us one of the supreme artists of our time. His conducting (if I may be permitted to judge him by phonograph records, since I heard Casals conduct in public only once, and the memory of that performance is not very vivid in my mind) has the stamp of profound musicianship, integrity, taste, discipline. But it is as a violoncellist that he raises the music he performs beyond sheer competence and musical authenticity, to Alpine peaks of greatness.

To many of us the memory of Casals performing the concertos of Haydn or Dvořák, or combining with Harold Bauer in a concert of Beethoven sonatas at Town Hall, or reading the Bach solo sonatas and suites in his own recitals, remain experiences never to be forgotten. His technique! It is as much a part of him as breathing, and comes from him as naturally. He has evolved his own system of fingering and bowing which make everything he plays seem simplified. His tone! It pours from his instrument opulently, but never sugary. The style!

It is that of a profound scholar and an aristocrat—every effect, every shade so subtly realized that one forgets the interpreter in the contemplation of a profound artistic expression. His sense for architectonic construction! "This magician," wrote Diran Alexanian, famous French teacher and violoncellist, "forces you to anticipate what is coming in the same way that he makes you remember what is past. In his playing, every note that is not a forecast is a memory. . . . Each detail has had attention, but the details are graded according to their importance."

He is the poet of his instrument; of few artists can this be said with equal justification. One recalls, for example, his performances of the *Adagio* movement of the Haydn concerto, or the *Adagio affettuoso* movement of the Brahms F-major sonata. Other cellists can bring to this music a wealth of tone and feeling. But only a supreme artist like Casals can, with the utmost of reserve, without torturing a figure or retarding a phrase, convert such "poems" into piercing, tragic utterances, ennobled by the simplicity of the expression.

Casals has the independence and courage and integrity of the supreme artist. France was not sympathetic to the sonatas of Brahms. Nevertheless Casals played them (the box office notwithstanding!), and played them so frequently that France, too, learned to appreciate the beauty of the music. If a famous orchestra leader slighted his beloved Dvořák concerto and asked him to make a substitution, he preferred not to make an appearance at all to changing the music.

Most important, however, have been Casals' efforts in bringing recognition to the great solo sonatas and suites of Johann Sebastian Bach.

While he was still in his adolescence, Casals—rummaging through some music in a second-hand shop in Barcelona—came across some copies of Bach's solo suites for violoncello. These works had almost never been performed by cellists, who regarded them (if they regarded them at all) as only good exercise material. To Casals, the Bach music opened a new world. From that day, Bach's music for the violoncello became his religion. He devoted his magnificent zeal and devotion to studying these works, analyzing phrase by phrase, bar by bar, until he felt that he could give it the performance they required. Then, on his concert tours, he set out to propagandize this music, playing it frequently in the face of criticism, boredom and the despair of his concert managers. He played it until, at last, the world saw through his eyes the majesty of Bach's music.

If Mendelssohn rediscovered for the world the *St. Matthew Passion* and Joseph Joachim the violin sonatas and suites, so Pablo Casals can be said to have restored

to the music world the solo sonatas and suites for violoncello.

3

The Casals family was one of the social pillars of the
small Catalonian town of Vendrell, Tarragona, re-
spected by all the townspeople. The father, Carles Casals,
was organist at Church, a teacher of singing and the
piano, and a respectable composer. He stemmed from
proud Catalonian stock; the mother was also partly Catalonian.

On December 29, 1876, another child was born to the
family. He was christened Pablo. He was a musical child.
From his father he received instruction in singing and
composition almost in his crib, and in his fourth year he
already sang in the parish church. The Gregorian chants
which he heard and sang in Church were his first forceful
musical impressions. At six, he supplemented his study of
the piano with that of the organ and began to write music.
At seven he began the study of the violin.

Playfully, Carles Casals used to tell his wife that they
had been blessed with another Mozart!

This enormous preoccupation with music did not bar
Pablo from the more normal life of a child. He was
small and slight, but healthy. He made friendships easily
and was well liked by the children of his own age. He

loved the outdoors; no less enthusiastically than his companions did he indulge in athletics. He was, as a matter of fact, a splendid runner and high-jumper.

But music was a world of endless wonder to him. The farther he traveled, the more he yearned to explore.

When he was ten, there took place in his town a Christmas performance of a pastorale-play. The music for this spectacle was found unsatisfactory, and father Casals was asked to prepare a new score. For this assignment, the father enlisted the collaboration of his talented young son. Together, they wrote more than a dozen musical numbers, which became so popular that—as we are informed by Casals' biographer, Lillian Littlehales [1] —some of these pieces are still sung by the townspeople.

Shortly after this, Pablo Casals heard a violoncello for the first time. The Catholic Center of Vendrell arranged a concert by instrumentalists, one of whom was José Garcia, a well known violoncellist from Barcelona. Hardly had the concert begun, when Pablo pointed a finger at the cello and urged his father to give him lessons on that instrument. Thus Pablo received his first instruction on the cello from his father. But his progress was so swift that other instruction was necessary. It was, finally, decided to send Pablo to Barcelona and have him enroll at the Municipal School where he could study

---

[1] *Pablo Casals*, by Lillian Littlehales. New York, 1929.

not only harmony and counterpoint but also the cello under José Garcia himself. Pablo was eleven years old when he entered the school. For three years he worked hard at his studies and won several prizes in theory and composition.

To support himself during his three years of study at the Municipal School, Pablo Casals played in a trio which performed every evening in a café-house outside of Barcelona. The trio performed the usual café-house repertoire of light music. But Pablo was even then too fine a musician to conform rigidly to a stereotyped repertoire. Before long he introduced in his programs selections from the great classics. Then he prevailed upon the manager of the café to permit him one evening in which to feature only the best music. That evening soon became famous throughout Barcelona. The city's *intelligenzia*— musicians, writers, painters, actors—made the café-house their weekly rendezvous on the evening when Casals featured musical masterpieces. One of these visitors was the famous Spanish composer, Isaac Albéniz, who immediately interested himself in the young musician and from that time on became his devoted friend.

It was at this time that Pablo Casals made his Bach discovery. He visited a Barcelona music shop and was rummaging through a pile of second-hand music in his search for some good music to feature on his programs when, as he himself has written, "my attention was suddenly arrested by some unaccompanied suites of Bach for cello. I forgot entirely the reason of my visit to the shop and could only stare at this music which nobody had told me about. Sometimes even now, when I look at the covers of that old music, I see again the interior of that old and musty shop with its faint smell of the sea. I took the suites home and read and reread them. For twelve years after that, I studied and worked every day at them. I was nearly twenty-five before I had the courage to play one of them in public."

Isaac Albéniz, who grew attached to the young musician, soon advised him to abandon Barcelona and leave for Madrid, where there were greater opportunities for a young musician.

Equipped with glowing letters of introduction from Isaac Albéniz and Fernandez Arbós, Casals left for Madrid where he performed successfully at the royal palace and soon found a generous and interested patron in Count Morphy. In Madrid he pursued study with greater assiduity than ever before—composition, under Tomas Breton, and the cello under Jesus de Monasterio (the latter of whom—as Casals had frequently confessed—exerted the most powerful influence over his artistic growth).

Through Count Morphy, Casals received a pension from the Queen enabling him to study at Brussels under the celebrated theorist, Gevaert. Gevaert was too old to accept private pupils, and he advised Casals to proceed to Paris. But first he urged him to visit the cello class at the Conservatory and play before the professor. At the class, the professor called on Casals to perform. "What can you play, my young Spaniard?" the professor asked him. "Anything," answered the young musician with cool self-assurance. The professor snickered; so did the class. "*Anything?*" The professor enumerated a few of the representative concertos for the cello, then some of the less famous ones. Casals said he could play them all. "Very well," said the professor acidly, "play anything you wish and show us if you are really as remarkable as you say."

Casals, in recalling this incident, remarked that the stinging tongue of the professor, coupled with the snickering and the laughter of the class, determined him to give an exceptional performance. He played as he had probably never played before. When he finished, the professor took him aside and said: "You are truly remarkable. You must study under me." To which Casals coolly answered: "I don't like you or your attitude. You have treated me so badly that I will not stay with you another minute." And without another word, he left the classroom.

He stayed two days in Brussels, and then left for Paris.

If Brussels had been discouraging, what then could be said of Paris where Casals met hardship, starvation and apathy? For Count Morphy was displeased at the move —and his pension was withdrawn. Through the influence of a friend he secured some work in a vaudeville house, the salary from which—meager though it was—kept him from starvation. The work was taxing and undermined his strength. "Every day I had to walk miles to and from this work with my violoncello under my arm. My mother eked out with sewing the few francs I earned. There were not only the two of us to keep but a little baby boy, too young for my mother to have left in Spain. After a few weeks I became ill with the strain and there was nothing left but to return to Spain."

Back in Barcelona, Casals confronted good fortune for the first time in his life. His former teacher, José Garcia, had resigned from the Municipal School and had left for Buenos Aires. His post was now offered to Casals.

He plunged into a delirium of musical activity. He taught at the Municipal School, played the violoncello in churches, and became the first cellist of the Opera orchestra in Barcelona. He formed his own string-quartet, which gave successful public performances. During the summer—when the musical activity relaxed in Barcelona—he played in a fashionable Casino of a small Portuguese town.

At the end of one summer, on his way back from Portugal to Barcelona, Casals stopped off at Madrid where, for the first time in his career, he gave a public performance with a symphony orchestra. He performed the Lalo Concerto in D-minor with Tomas Breton conducting the orchestra. His performance was so successful that the Queen bestowed upon him the Order of Carlos III.

For two years, Casals worked hard in Barcelona, saved money, and practised industriously on his cello. He was developing and growing as an artist. Then, having accumulated a comfortable bank account, he decided to abandon his work in Barcelona and to visit Paris a second time—perhaps now to enter officially a career as concert artist.

He arrived in Paris in the autumn of 1899 with a letter of introduction from Count Morphy to Charles Lamoureux, conductor of a famous orchestra bearing his name, and one of the most influential musicians in France. At the time Lamoureux was absorbed in the work of preparing *Tristan und Isolde* for performance in Paris. When Casals arrived at Lamoureux's home, the conductor was busy working at the piano. Lamoureux interrupted his work long enough to give his visitor a casual greeting. "Come tomorrow," he said brusquely. "And bring your cello." The next day Casals returned and played. Lamoureux—who had not interrupted his work even while Casals was playing—suddenly raised his head from his papers. Motionless, he listened, his face beaming. At the end of Casals' performance he embraced him and exclaimed: "But you are extraordinary! You must play at my very next concert."

In October of 1899, Casals made his début in Paris with the Lamoureux Orchestra and was a sensation. Overnight Casals became famous. Engagements from all parts of Europe and America poured in upon him.

A few months after this début, the man who had discovered him and first revealed him to the world, Charles Lamoureux, died. "With his death passed my days of poverty and struggle."

4

Thereafter, Casals' career was one of uninterrupted triumph. He concertized throughout the world—visiting America first in 1901, and then again in 1904—and saw his reputation swell prodigiously. The world soon recognized him as one of its most precious artists, and has honored him lavishly. His own government has bestowed upon him innumerable decorations and awards. From Germany he received the degree of Science and Arts; from Austria-Hungary, the Cross of the Commander of Francis Joseph; from France, the Legion of

Honor, the Palme Academique and the Cross of L'Instruction publique; from Italy, membership in the Royal Academy of St. Cecilia of Rome; from Portugal, the order of Santiago da Espada; from Rumania, the Commandership of the Crown; and from London the Beethoven gold medal which had previously been bestowed upon Brahms, Rubinstein, Joachim and Liszt.

For many years, Casals divided not only his residence, but the major share of his music-making between Paris and Barcelona. In Paris he not only gave his solo performances and sonata recitals, but he also combined with Jacques Thibaud and Alfred Cortot in trio performances which were often the high points of the concert season. In Barcelona he founded his orchestra, and shared his efforts between the cello and the baton.

At one time, Casals seriously thought of abandoning the cello. He had married the American singer, Susan Metcalfe, in 1914. For several seasons he appeared as an accompanist to his wife in *Lieder* recitals. For a long time, he seriously contemplated giving up his own career to further that of his wife. But, fortunately, he never made the fatal decision.

The truth is that Casals does not like playing the cello, detests extensive concertizing, and would prefer to devote all his time and zeal to conducting. An interesting anecdote illustrates this forcefully. Once, climbing Mt.

Tamalpais, he saw a huge rock descending upon him. He made an impetuous move to avoid the descending rock, but in doing so caught a finger of his left hand and crushed it. The first thought that came to his mind was: "Thank God, I won't have to play the cello again!"

Fortunately for the world of music, this accident did not end Casals' career as a cellist. But he has always relieved the tension and strain of extensive concert work as a virtuoso with guest performances as a conductor. He has directed the major orchestras in Vienna, Paris, London, Rome, Berlin, Prague, Zurich and Buenos Aires. In 1922, he conducted the New York Symphony Orchestra at Carnegie Hall for one performance.

Conducting is no less arduous a task for Casals than playing the cello; it is, as a matter of fact, an occupation that exhausts him physically and mentally. But musicianship as profound as that of Casals refuses to be hemmed in by the limited boundaries of virtuoso performances. Conducting offers Casals an inexhaustibly rich medium of self-expression, such as he cannot find in his cello. His ambition, therefore, is some day to make the transition from cello to baton complete and irrevocable.

Before that day comes, it is to be hoped that Pablo Casals returns to America to refresh our memory of his incomparable playing. It has been more than a decade

Joseph Szigeti

since he last concertized in this country. During his absence, we have heard here many admirable, even extraordinary cellists. But there are no substitutes for
Casals. The gap he has left in our concert life cannot be
adequately filled in our time unless he himself returns to
fill it.

XII: SZIGETI

CHAPTER TWELVE

JOSEPH SZIGETI

THE art of Joseph Joachim is today, probably, most closely approximated in the violin playing of Joseph Szigeti. Curiously enough, Szigeti—like his distinguished predecessor—is.Hungarian by nationality, and a Jew by religion. And, paradoxically enough, both violinists are characteristically un-Hungarian and un-Jewish in their art. With the Hungarian we associate the hot blood of the *csardas;* with the Jew, indulgence in emotion and sentiment. Yet Szigeti—like Joachim before him—is most strongly guided not by emotional impulses but by his keen and trenchant intellect. His performance is always a studied art, as carefully and fastidiously conceived in every detail as a symphony in the hands of a great conductor.

It may be recalled that when Joachim visited Russia at the prime of his career, he was greeted with a reserve that approached apathy. To Russian music lovers, accustomed to the heady wine of Wieniawski, Joachim's playing was as frigid, as coldly calculated as the solo sonatas of Bach which he had resurrected and which, to the Russians at the time, appeared a downright bore. It may also be recalled that when Szigeti gave his first concerts in America he was frequently greeted with a similar condemnation. His tone, some said, lacked the human quality of tenderness. His style, some said further, was too restrained and reserved. He held his emotion too much in check. He was, in short, too much the mind, too little the heart.

To some of us, who consider Szigeti an artist of the first importance, one of whom we are most proud, such accusations are as unjustified as those which Joachim received in Russia. To some of us, Szigeti is quite in a class by himself. An art such as his—so penetratingly analytical, so beautifully sculptured in every line and curve— can never have a mass appeal. Essentially, Szigeti's art is for the discriminating. He is—so they will tell you—a violinist's violinist.

If, when he plays at Carnegie Hall, he does not pack the hall to the doors as one or two other violinists do, he can at least boast of having a most fastidious audience before him. Concert-violinists are there in droves, to study his style in all its varied subtlety, to derive through his insight a new conception of great violin music.

They know that at Szigeti's concerts they will hear programs that are musically significant throughout, programs which never cater to popular taste, which are intelligently balanced, including the dessert of novelty together with the roast-beef of classical music. For Szigeti, more than any other violinist since Joachim, has made of program-building an art in itself. And there are few concert violinists who will not concede that Szigeti has profoundly influenced the art of program-making.

A Szigeti program is always an adventure for the music lover. At one time, in New York, he gave a series of concerts which spanned the history of violin music; avenues in violin music, long closed, were then opened by him. Such rarities as a *Divertimento* by Mozart (who had ever heard of a violinist featuring an orchestral *Divertimento* on a recital program?), and an unknown concerto by Tartini were introduced by him at another of his recitals, with the assistance of a chamber orchestra. At a more recent concert he invited Benny Goodman to appear with him for the world première at Béla Bartók's *Rhapsody*, for clarinet, violin and piano. These are only a few indications that a Szigeti program is always alive, novel and ingeniously contrived.

Concert violinists who come to Szigeti's concerts understand that if, as in the Brahms concerto, Szigeti adopts a style that is often acrid and harsh, it is only because he has found in the work a strength and toughness of fiber; also that he can play Schubert with sensuous and soaring lyricism. In certain modern works, Szigeti's playing actually approaches the ugly, in the stridency of tones he produces on the violin—as, for example, in the Prokofieff First Violin Concerto, which he introduced to the world, and of which he is, as Prokofieff himself has said, the greatest interpreter. But in the classical sonata, he is the purist, adhering strictly to the classical line. And in the classical sonata, Szigeti adopts a chamber music style in which the virtuoso is forgotten in the beautiful adjustment of the two instruments.

In short, concert violinists understand that Szigeti's style changes miraculously almost with every composition. For technique to Szigeti does not consist merely in the ability to produce a full rich tone, or to play a complicated passage with neatness of execution. Technique is much more than that to Szigeti. It is the ability to adapt his equipment to the different styles of different composers.

The type of audience that comes to hear Szigeti play is a tribute to his art. Equally eloquent a tribute to the great scope of his art is the eagerness with which modern composers prepare works especially for him. Hamilton Harty and Alfredo Casella have dedicated their violin concertos to him; Busoni's is permanently associated with his name. Dedications to him likewise appear on Eugene Ysaye's violin sonata, Bloch's *Nuit exotique*, Templeton Strong's *Poem*, Saminsky's *Hamavdil*, Béla Bartók's

Rhapsody for violin and orchestra and the *Rhapsody* for clarinet, violin and piano (the last-named, jointly, to him and Benny Goodman), Joseph Achron's *Stempenyu Suite*, Alexander Tansman's *Suite* and Prokofieff's *Chant sans paroles*. Ernest Bloch waited more than a year for the world première of his violin concerto so that Szigeti might give it its first performance.

For the great modern composers realize that when Szigeti plays their music, their inmost fancy, their slightest intentions become fully realized; that their music is not exploited for the glorification of the artist and his technique, but that artist and technique become the humble servants of the music.

2

Look at the man; notice his fine and sensitive face, the high, majestic forehead the height of which is accentuated by the sparse growth of hair, the far-seeing eyes, the soft slopes of the cheek. Talk to him, listen to him discourse on aesthetics, science or literature . . . and you will gain an insight into the aristocratic personality which is the source of his profound and moving art.

His height gives him a suggestion of awkwardness, even when he is on the platform. But, as you watch him more closely, you notice that his body is lithe and supple, and his gestures (particularly those of his hands) are graceful. As he talks to you, he speaks with a soft, well-modulated voice, which he never raises even when excited. He likes to talk, and—at the slightest provocation —will grow expansive over some beautiful painting he has seen, a great book he has read, his most recent travels, of which he never seems to grow tired.

His home is in Paris, a spacious apartment on the Boulevard Haussmann, cluttered with books, music, paintings, and mementos of his many trips. There is very little of home life for Szigeti, who is continually traveling, filling extensive concert engagements. But a few months during the summer, which are spent in a secluded corner of the Swiss Alps, and a few scattered weeks in the winter, at his Paris home, are religiously set aside to permit Szigeti to live quietly with his wife and daughter.

Szigeti has known two great musical influences early in his career. To these two influences he freely expresses his indebtedness. One of these was the violinist Joseph Joachim, whom he heard play when he was very young; that was an experience which Szigeti never forgot. The other musician was the great pianist, composer and conductor, Ferruccio Busoni, at one time a personal friend of Szigeti. These two great artists—their integrity, idealism, their intellectual approach to their art—directed Szigeti's artistic course.

Szigeti has also expressed indebtedness to Béla Bartók, whom he first met about fourteen or so years ago and who has since become a personal friend. The folk elements in Bartók's composition have exerted a strong influence on Szigeti, who some time ago transcribed some of Bartók's Hungarian folk-tunes for the violin. Szigeti has frequently appeared in joint recitals with Bartók, both in Europe and America, in programs featuring the composer's music.

3

Joseph Szigeti was born in Budapest on September 5, 1892. Showing an early aptitude for the violin, he was given instruction first by his father and then by his uncle. He outgrew these preliminary studies quickly, and was placed under the expert guidance of the great Hungarian violinist and teacher, Jenö Hubay.

When Szigeti was twelve years old, his teacher brought him to the great Joachim who accompanied the boy at the piano as he performed the violin concerto of Beethoven. The performance was sufficiently distintinguished for Joachim to encourage him in an artistic career. One year later, Szigeti made his début at the

Royal Academy of Budapest. And two years after that, at the age of fifteen, he played in Berlin, Dresden, and finally came to England.

Szigeti remained in England six years, concertizing extensively in London and the provinces, sometimes in joint recitals with the singer, Melba, the pianist, Bachaus, and the great composer Busoni. Szigeti's playing received praise throughout England. "He has the *diablerie* which must have been Paganini's secret," the London *Times* wrote. Another critic compared his interpretations to a Benvenuto Cellini masterpiece, in its perfect balance and beauty.

In 1912, Szigeti's concert tour brought him out of England to Berlin and Paris, where he successfully featured the Busoni violin concerto, dedicated to him by the composer. In Paris his concert was organized by the foremost intellectual figures then in the city, including Gabriel D'Annunzio, Isidor Philipp, Moritz Moszkowski, Charles Widor and Rainer Maria Rilke. After the concert (at which the featured composition was once again the Busoni concerto), a banquet took place at the old café-restaurant Henri. A piano was brought to the first floor, and there—when the dinner was over—Busoni played his formidable piano work, the *Fantasia Contrappuntistica*, to his many disciples.

222

His concert tour continued. His reputation grew, not by sudden inflation, but slowly and steadily. They began to speak of his beautiful conceptions, of his exquisite etchings of the great musical works.

In 1917, Szigeti succeeded the celebrated Henri Marteau as professor of the class of violin virtuosity at the Geneva Conservatory. He held this position with distinction till 1924.

Leopold Stokowski, then conductor of the Philadelphia Symphony Orchestra, heard him play in Europe and invited him to America. In the autumn of 1925, Szigeti made his début as soloist with the Philadelphia Symphony Orchestra in Philadelphia, playing the concerto of Beethoven. A week later, he repeated this performance in New York.

Some of the critics were cool to him because his tone did not have the fullness and wealth of Heifetz's, and his interpretation the charm of Kreisler's. But a few critics recognized that Szigeti was an individualist who must not be measured by the yardstick of existing standards, that his style was uniquely his own. They recognized that with Szigeti, the design of the music, the musical content of a composition, were of first importance; not the minute elements of violin playing. Olin Downes compared Szigeti to Eugene Ysaye because of his "breadth and generosity of style." Another critic proclaimed him "an individuality—a violinist whose art is more than an episode of a season."

However, it would be wrong to call Szigeti's début in America sensational. He was not immediately numbered among the elect of contemporary violinists—except by a limited handful of discerning music lovers. Passing seasons, however, brought renewed contact with Szigeti's art; and renewed contact disclosed the infinite variety of his playing, and the true nobility of his interpretations. He was, it was soon learned, the consummate artist who, as Paul Stefan pointed out, "represents with equal completeness the classic greatness and the modern spirit of violin playing."

Szigeti has his devoted followers throughout the world. His audience exists wherever music is played. His concert tours are extensive: From May 1931 to May 1933, for example, he encircled the globe twice, giving more than two hundred performances. In Tokio he played five consecutive nights; and seven consecutive nights in Buenos Aires. He was invited twelve times to the Soviet Union, where he has been accorded one of the greatest receptions he has received anywhere. In 1938, he was so triumphantly received in South Africa that a schedule of twelve concerts was expanded to nineteen.

The foremost honors have fallen to him. In France, he

was awarded the Legion of Honor. In Belgium, he was made Commander of the Order of Leopold. He has received the Officer's Cross of the Hungarian *Ordre pour le merité*. In Japan, he was the recipient of the Jiji Shimpo Gold Medal.

But perhaps the greatest honor which is his is the devoted enthusiasm of his followers, musicians who remain staunchly faithful to him, who hear him whenever he chooses to play, and who derive from his playing an aesthetic pleasure such as they get only from a handful of living artists—from Toscanini, Pablo Casals, Lotte Lehmann or Gieseking.

Walter Gieseking

XIII: GIESEKING

CHAPTER THIRTEEN

WALTER GIESEKING

IT IS said that when his manager first brought Walter Gieseking to America, he refused to publicize the rhapsodic reviews which Gieseking had received in Europe. Such reviews, the manager felt, would never be believed of a completely unknown artist by incredulous New York. It was far better strategy, thought the manager, to have Gieseking come to this country unheralded, to have his art burst upon the critics without the forewarning of elaborate publicity.

And so, when Gieseking gave his first American concert on January 10, 1926, there were few in the audience who knew much about him. The better informed—those who kept their fingers alert on the pulse of European musical activity—knew vaguely that his playing had been well praised and that Hull's *Dictionary of Music and Musicians* had spoken of him as a specialist in modern music. Others in the audience were not even familiar with his name—which, indicative of his obscurity, had been misspelled the day before in the *New York Times* advertisement!

It was a typical Gieseking program: some Bach—the B-flat major Partita; three sonatas of Domenico Scarlatti; a major Schumann work—the *Kreisleriana;* and a preponderance of Debussy—the entire first book of preludes, as a matter of fact. An extraordinary program for a pianist about to make his American début! No fireworks; no sure-fire staples of the piano repertoire; no Beethoven, Chopin, or Liszt. Only the less familiar in piano literature.

Yet, though the program promised adventure, the critics who came to report the concert could hardly anticipate much more in Gieseking than a run-of-the-mill pianist. However, they must have suddenly stiffened in their seats when the first few phrases of Bach were enunciated, must have pricked up their ears with no little incredulity. The enormous frame of the man, which crouched ape-like over the keyboard, was producing qualities of which few, if any, suspected the piano was capable. Suddenly the piano became as sensitive and refined in sound as a harpsichord; the delicate music acquired a fragile-like framework, so diaphonous, so sensitive, that it almost seemed it might collapse at the slightest touch. The tones came crisply, glisteningly. And what pianist could duplicate a *pianissimo* such as Gieseking was urging from the piano—a *pianissimo* as elusive as the faintest whisper, yet with body and substance; it was a *pianissimo* such as de Pachmann produced when he was at the height of his career.

As the concert developed, the miracles increased. From delicacy, Gieseking could pass—in Schumann—to a fortissimo of orchestral sonority, rich and luscious in texture. Not only could he pluck a crisp staccato from the piano, but he could also draw a beautiful singing legato, in which the melody lifted and soared. He could, at alternate moments, make the piano strum like Segovia's guitar, sing like Casals' cello. The piano, at other moments, acquired the percussive thunder of tympani.

And his Debussy! For the first time, it seemed, the true nature of Debussy's piano music—so long approximated by other artists—became revealed. For the first time, it seemed, the piano seemed capable of the shimmering colors, the subtle tints and hues, the vague and remote suggestions of sights and sounds which the composer had expressed in his preludes.

That début was an unforgettable experience for the small audience fortunate enough to have been present. "Mr. Geiseking is an exceptional pianist and needed only the opening measure or two of the first number to prove it," reported Francis D. Perkins in the *Herald Tribune*. "The skill, neatness and polish of his technique are truly remarkable. He played Bach and Scarlatti with a fluent evenness, an exceptional nicety and clarity of detail producing perfectly cameos of sound. Correspondingly nicety and subtle variation characterized his shading." "The introspection, the poignancy, the humor, the whimsy of Schumann . . . were conveyed with the touch and technical proficiency of a true artist," further commented Olin Downes in the *New York Times*.

As Gieseking's appearances in America became more frequent, the chorus of praise swelled among the critics. They referred to him as "the greatest living interpreter of Scarlatti, Debussy and the modern composers"; they rhapsodized over the "power, beauty and fire of his playing," which was the "model of unerring taste allied with consummate sensibility and superb effectiveness."

Yet, for all this acclaim, Gieseking, like Szigeti, has no large audience to overflow the concert hall when he plays. Essentially, Gieseking is the pianist's pianist, just as Szigeti is the violinist's violinist. Gieseking's appeal, I am afraid, must always be limited. His is no bravura style to sweep audiences into a frenzy of appreciation with breath-taking display of technique. His art is too subtle to take one by storm. He does not even feature the music demanded by the majority of concert goers. Until recently, Chopin and Liszt were never featured by him at all. And the music of Debussy and the modern composers has never been known to fill concert halls with admiring enthusiasts.

But to a discriminating audience, sufficiently sensitive to recognize the far-reaching implications of his art, Gieseking stands with the great interpreters of our day. I think that there should be small question of that.

Gieseking is not merely a great interpreter of piano music. More than that, he has revolutionized piano technique. He has brought to the instrument effects and qualities which seem to have been explored by him for the first time. These effects he has evolved after many years of experiment, years of painful and untiring practice and indefatigable application. As he once told me: "I have worked for hours in applying different degrees of pressure upon the keys, until I have become a complete master of my muscles and can produce a fragile strum by the most fragmentary contact of finger-tip and piano key. The patience required is enormous. But this effort will be more than repaid by the attainment of a touch so sensitive that it can produce sounds of the most exquisite delicacy. . . . I also worked incessantly with the pedals in an attempt to create new qualities of sound. Take, for example, Debussy's *La Cloche à travers les feuilles* in which appears a passage to be played—so we are told by the composer—like a 'breath on the window-pane.' By subtle manipulation of the pedals, and by a carefully sensitized touch the pianist can actually produce a sound so hazy and misty that it can approximate the effect for which Debussy was groping."

2

Each time Gieseking plays there is the shock of the unexpected in seeing a huge form crouch over the piano, attack the keyboard with massive hands, and then draw from the instrument sounds of exquisite refinement. It is difficult, meeting Gieseking personally for the first time, to associate his appearance with his profession. In build (he is six feet tall) he resembles an athlete. His frame is large and well developed. His face has strength of character—the type of face capable, one feels, of making important decisions quickly at a bank president's desk. Not even the eyes betray the artist in him, for they, too, are strong and assertive.

Even his temperament is more like a banker's than a musician's. He is devoid of eccentricities and moods. In everything he does, he is calculated, practical, analytical. His diversions, perhaps, best reveal the man: he likes gardening, tinkering with machinery, climbing mountains or swimming. He is of the earth—not somewhere in the clouds. Only one hobby of his seems out of character with the rest of the man: he is a passionate entomologist. In his music studio in Wiesebaden he possesses one of the rarest collection of butterflies in the world. At one time he interrupted a concert tour in America to take a ten day holiday in Florida to catch rare specimens of butterfly. At another time he stopped in the midst of an outdoor performance of a piano quintet when a particularly desirable moth flew past his head. He caught it.

His home is in Wiesebaden, Germany, where he lives with his wife and daughters, Freia and Justa. It is a beautiful modernistic home constructed of steel and glass which, situated on a hill, is removed from the city proper. Here, during the summer, Gieseking conducts special classes in piano playing, in cooperation with his one-time teacher, Karl Leimar; and here, piano pupils from all parts of Europe come for the final touches to their training before embarking on concert tours.

3

Walter Gieseking was born in Lyons, France, on November 5, 1895. His father, a physician well-known on the Italian Riviera where he enjoyed an extensive practice, was a lover of music. He could play the flute and piano with considerable skill.

His son, Walter, showed an interest in music at an early age, and began the study of the violin shortly after his fourth birthday. For three years Walter continued studying the violin, making satisfactory progress. But the piano interested Walter more, from the first. He had been diverting himself at the keyboard from earliest childhood, and as the years passed he found himself drawn to it more and more. At the age of seven, he firmly announced to his father his decision to abandon the violin for the piano. His father, too wise to discourage him, consented.

Walter Gieseking was sixteen years old when his family transferred its home from France to Germany— Hanover, specifically. Two events of major importance occurred to Gieseking after this transplantation. The first was his initial hearing of Debussy's piano music which (paradoxically!) had been an unknown world to him in France. He took to Debussy, studied him passionately, and derived from his music a true inspiration. The second major event was his entrance into the Conservatory of Hanover where that wise and eminent teacher of the piano, Karl Leimer (today Gieseking's friend and partner) took him under his personal care. These were years of intensive study, years of absorption in musical experiences and the mastery of piano technique, years of fastidious dissection of musical literature. How quickly Gieseking developed during these years was proved in 1915, when he gave a series of six concerts in Hanover in which he performed all the thirty-two piano sonatas by Beethoven. Surely no Conservatory pupil has ever equaled a feat such as this! The opinion of many who heard these concerts was that even few mature artists could equal Gieseking's technical fluency and artistic insight.

When he was eighteen, Gieseking began to tour neighboring German towns as concert pianist. His success tempted him to consider seriously the possibility of a concert career. The War, however, temporarily interrupted his concert work. For two years, between 1916 and 1918, Gieseking served in the German army, helping his adopted country by succoring the morale of his fellow soldiers. He played for them lusty German dance music on the piano, or on the violin, or on the viola, or on any other musical instrument that was at hand.

The property of the Gieseking family, which remained in Lyons during the War, was confiscated by the French government, leaving the Gieseking family destitute. When the War ended, Gieseking was entirely dependent on his music for a livelihood. He returned to Hanover, set up shop as a teacher of the piano (charging as little as forty cents for a lesson), and let it be known that he was available for concert engagements. These were not slow in coming; his impressive performances of 1915 had not been forgotten.

Fortuitously, post-War Germany manifested an enormous appetite for modern music. And Gieseking had, ever since settling in Germany, been an ardent proponent of the modern composer. He made a concert appearance in Hanover featuring the music of Debussy and modern German composers. There were other concert appearances and invitations from other German cities. His reputation began to grow. In Paris he was acclaimed. It was not long before, in Europe, they began to speak of Gieseking as the foremost interpreter of modern music.

But the music world soon learned that Gieseking's art was not one-sided. If he was a great interpreter of the modern style, he was no less remarkable in his performances of Scarlatti, Bach, Beethoven or Schumann. And it was his imaginative recreation of the great music of the past, even more than his understanding of and sympathy for the modern composer, which has placed Gieseking, in the opinion of so many discriminating music lovers, among the great virtuosos of today.

XIV: PINZA

CHAPTER FOURTEEN

EZIO PINZA

WHEN Ezio Pinza made his American début in 1926, one critic astutely referred to him as a "young Chaliapin." The remark was prophetic. Today, with Chaliapin dead, no one appears more likely to succeed him than Pinza. The Metropolitan Opera House realized this strongly —for, when it planned a revival of Moussorgsky's *Boris Godounov* for its 1938–1939 season, it selected Pinza for the rôle so long immortalized by the Russian bass.

The more one studies Pinza's performances, the more forcefully one becomes conscious that he is Chaliapin's inevitable successor. Like Chaliapin, Pinza is much more than a great singer. He has a magnificent voice, of course —extraordinary for its texture, range, volume, flexibility. But with Pinza, as with his predecessor, the voice is only one of several important elements of his art. Pinza is also a great dramatic actor who vibrantly recreates each rôle he performs. It used to be said of Chaliapin—and, I believe, by no one less than Stanislavsky of the Moscow Art Theatre—that had he never chosen Opera, he would have been one of the world's great actors. This might also be said of Pinza. Each of Pinza's operatic characterizations is as meticulously drawn as Hamlet is in the hands of John Gielgud or Maurice Evans.

When Pinza studies a new rôle, the dramatic preparation is often more intensive than the musical. He buries himself in history to understand the setting and period in which his character moves. If the character is an historical one, he absorbs all existing biographies for a more intimate understanding of the person he is trying to recreate. He will go to the museum and pore over paintings of the period for a study of costumes, and even of facial expressions. For his Don Giovanni, for example, he made an intensive study of Velasquez. Then, when the character is vivid in his mind, he will experiment with gestures and facial expressions to intensify the dramatic situations in which his character becomes involved.

Watching Pinza on the stage as Don Giovanni, Frère Laurent, Lothario, King Dodon, Oroveso or Figaro is as much an experience for the eye as for the ear. He is a dominating figure on the stage, as compelling and magnetic as Chaliapin used to be in his tremendous characterization of Boris. Every phase of the histrionic art has been mastered by Pinza and has become servant to the character he is attempting to project. His make-up, of which he has made a science and an art; his gestures (has it ever been noticed what eloquent use he makes of

Ezio Pinza
in Don Giovanni

his hands to accentuate a dramatic moment?); his carefully thought out analysis of a character which make each of his rôles an integrated conception—these are qualities in Pinza's art no less striking than the authenticity, musicianship and charm of his singing.

In one respect he has gone even beyond Chaliapin—in his amazing versatility. He has sung almost every major bass rôle in operatic literature, and being a thorough artist, has sung them all remarkably well. Italian opera is, of course, his *forte*. But he has adapted himself with incredible plasticity to the varying styles of French, German and Russian operas as well. His repertoire today includes more than fifty operas in almost every style of operatic writing. Who else on the operatic stage can boast of having sung so successfully in such varied operas as *Die Meistersinger, Tristan und Isolde, Mignon, Faust, Lakmé, Don Giovanni, The Marriage of Figaro, Aïda, La Juive, Barber of Seville, Norma, Le Coq d'or* and *Boris Godounov?*

2

Ezio Pinza was born in Rome on May 18, 1892, the youngest son of seven children. His father was a lumber dealer.

Pinza had been born so puny that he was not expected

to live. Two days passed after his birth without even a christening name having been selected for him. At the end of the second day it appeared that he might survive. It was then that a friend of the family suggested (perhaps in jest) that he be called Ezio, a pagan name forbidden by the Church. The name was accepted by the father.

A music profession for Ezio was remotest from his father's mind, who had hopes of making his son a civil engineer. In Ravenna, to which the Pinza family transferred its home when Ezio was two years old, the boy began his studies preparatory to a training in engineering. But engineering was distasteful to Ezio. When he was seventeen, he abandoned his studies to become—of all things!—a professional bicycle racer. He entered in cross country competitions and in six-day bicycle races—but only once won second prize.

He tells us today that at one time, immediately after a race, he was in a shower when suddenly he burst into song. He had had, up to the time, no musical education; his only experience as a singer had been in an amateur choral club. One of his friends heard him, and laughingly told him he was a much better singer than a bicycle racer, then more soberly asked him why he did not pursue the study of music. This was the first time that Pinza thought seriously of music.

244

He liked to sing, and he liked music. His failures as a professional bicycle racer made him further receptive to the idea. He decided to turn to a new career. When he was eighteen he began the study of singing under Maestro Ruzza. Then, upon the death of Ruzza, Pinza became a pupil at the Conservatory of Bologna under Maestro Vezzani. He learned quickly and was soon ready for an operatic début. But the War interrupted his career. "For four years," Pinza today says, "I kept my voice on ice. I mean this not only metaphorically but literally as well—for I was a member of the Italian artillery, fighting eight thousand feet above sea level in the Alps."

When the War ended Pinza returned to singing and made his début in the Teatro Reale dell' Opera in Rome. His rôle was that of King Mark in *Tristan und Isolde*.

He remained at the Teatro Reale for two years, growing rapidly as an artist. Then, after a short and successful engagement in Turin, he came to La Scala in Milan, to sing for three years under Toscanini. It was here that he acquired his great fame. His versatility and profound musicianship and inimitable operatic style aroused the admiration of all discriminating musicians. Toscanini himself considered Pinza one of his most capable performers. When, in 1924, Toscanini decided to give the world première of *Nerone*, by Boïto who had died a few years earlier (an event which drew to Milan music lovers from all parts of Europe), he chose Pinza for a principal rôle.

It was at La Scala that Gatti-Casazza heard Pinza sing and engaged him for the Metropolitan Opera House.

Pinza's début at the Metropolitan took place in 1926 in Spontini's *La Vestale*. His recognition was immediate. One critic, as has already been cited, spoke of him as a "young Chaliapin." Olin Downes reported that he was "a majestic figure on the stage; a bass of superb sonority and impressiveness."

There followed engagements in San Francisco and Chicago, then in London, Paris and South America, finally in Vienna and Salzburg. His popularity now became world wide, and few there were who would not concede him a position of major importance among the opera stars of the day. In the Salzburg festivals, for a few years, he sang in *The Marriage of Figaro* and *Don Giovanni*, and was generally considered one of the major personalities of the festival, and one of the great living basses.

3

Pinza is one of the handsomest singers in the Metropolitan Opera House—athletically built (over six feet tall, and weighing almost two hundred pounds), with

246

dark eyes, his dark hair now slightly touched by gray. His face is finely chiselled and Romanesque; the aquiline nose descends from almond-shaped eyes toward lips that are thin and firm. The eyes have characteristic Italian intensity. He dresses smartly, and shows a preference for vivid colors.

Pinza has a contagious joviality, is almost always in high spirits, and indulges frequently in jokes. Generally he is in a communicative mood. At the slightest encouragement, he will grow expansive about himself, his many diversions and pastimes. He is fond of photography. Sports are, probably, his major interest outside of music. He goes frequently to boxing matches. He likes to ski, ride the bicycle and, most of all, to drive an automobile (one summer he drove 12,000 miles in Europe). One hobby he has above all others: ancient Roman poison rings, of which he now has a formidable collection.

He will confess, somewhat diffidently, that there is in him a strong and uncontrollable vein of superstition. To this day he has retained the small and dingy dressing room at the Metropolitan Opera House which was assigned to him for his first appearance; he thinks it would break his luck to change. He believes that Friday and the number 13 are lucky for him. And he clings tenaciously to a luck-charm—a small, battered doll, which is his mascot everywhere and which always decorates his dressing table. That doll had been given to him many years ago by a young girl friend, but any more of his history, or the source of its unique powers, Pinza stubbornly refuses to disclose.

MEN AND WOMEN WHO MAKE MUSIC

XV: MENUHIN

CHAPTER FIFTEEN

YEHUDI MENUHIN

TWO years of retirement and study, on a ranch in the Santa Cruz mountains of California, was the transition marking the passing of Yehudi Menuhin from a prodigy-violinist to a full-fledged artist.

Yehudi Menuhin has some time ago passed his twenty-second birthday. He has outgrown the infectious charm of childhood; from precocity he has stepped into full maturity. Man's estate became his on the day he married Nola Nicholas of Australia, in London.

For too many prodigies, the step from childhood to maturity has proved fatal. It has brought them from fame to obscurity, from the adulation of a public to its indifference. For Yehudi, however, the age of twenty-two held no terrors. With each year following his phenomenal début, he found himself more securely established in fame, more maturely developed as an artist. With each year, his march through the world of music became more of a personal triumph. When, in 1937, he returned to the concert stage after an absence of two years, he emphasized once again his enormous appeal. At the box-office he established himself as the greatest musical attraction in the world! Artistically, he thrived equally well. The outstanding music critics, musicians, violin teachers hailed him as one of the foremost masters of his instrument.

Truth to tell, Yehudi Menuhin the man may no longer be looked upon as the picturesque chubby child prodigy whose audiences were delighted at the sight of a mere fledgling playing great music on a violin too large for him. But he has become something infinitely more important: he has become a great artist.

2

Today, Yehudi finds himself a world figure in music. His fame literally spans the globe. His career has been so generously studded with triumphs that they could easily crowd a normal lifetime of any other artist. Toward which of his many victories does this young artist today look back with the most exhilaration and nostalgia?

To that all-important first appearance in New York when, as a mere child, he played the Beethoven Concerto in Carnegie Hall and Mecca Temple to the accompaniment of the New York Symphony Society? Dressed in a white shirt with short sleeves, velvet knee breeches, socks and pumps, he was an unforgettable sight as he gave his violin to the concertmaster for tuning. He saw ladies in the boxes sobbing softly into their handkerchiefs, as, with chubby fingers, he drew exquisite sounds from his violin. He saw three thousand people rise spontaneously at the end of his performance to cheer him. He was lifted high, and kissed, by the conductor of the orchestra—Fritz Busch. . . . And the following morning, the critics joined in one chorus of praise to his genius. "When the bow touched the strings, it was evident that an exceptional musical intelligence and sensibility were behind the performance. . . . He felt, he conveyed very beautifully the poetry of the slow movement, and his playing of the finale was of refreshing taste and simplicity," wrote Olin Downes in the *New York Times*. "From the fingers of this child of ten," wrote Samuel Chotzinoff, "the Beethoven Concerto flowed in all its nobility, its repose, its thoughtful and subjective beauty. . . ."

Is it to his unforgettable début in Berlin that Yehudi today most frequently turns his roving memory? Rumors of his remarkable exploits had reached Berlin, but musicians and critics were incredulous; they would have to hear for themselves. He performed at one concert three of the most difficult concertos in musical literature (those of Beethoven and Brahms and one by Bach). There were tears and cheers and rapturous enthusiasm.

Some went so far as to say that they had not heard such playing since the days of Joachim. . . . But that début was especially memorable to him for quite another reason. After the concert a little man with electric eyes and bushy hair came to him backstage, lifted him high in his arms, and kissed him squarely on his hot cheek. "Today, Yehudi," the stranger said to him, "you have once again proved to me that there is a God in heaven!" The little man was Albert Einstein.

Or does Yehudi regard the day of November 14, 1931, as the most memorable of his life? It was then that, at the invitation of the city of Leipzig, he appeared with the Gewandhaus Orchestra on the occasion of the 150th anniversary of the great orchestra's origin. I shall permit a letter from Yehudi's father, Moshe—written to a personal friend shortly after the event—describe that day of triumph.

"After Yehudi had finished performing the Mendelssohn concerto, Bruno Walter, the conductor of the orchestra, was caught speechless, holding his hand to his heart. Finally, Mr. Walter cried out aloud: 'This is a miracle! This is Godly! This is genius of the highest order!'

"At the same time, the public was calling out Yehudi more than twenty times, and compelled him to play an encore (the very first time in the history of symphony

254

concerts in the Gewandhaus that an encore was given!).
Yehudi played a Bach solo sonata as an encore, another
thing that broke all rules. . . .

"A banquet was tendered Yehudi last night, at the
house of the president of the Gewandhaus, at which over
one hundred of Germany's greatest leaders in art, science,
music and politics came to do him honor. The great
Felix Mendelssohn's grandchildren were there to thank
Yehudi for his performance of their grandfather's concerto. Dr. Bumke, vice-president of the German republic and president of the Supreme Court of Germany, was
there, and delivered a speech which made my backbone
shiver. 'Do you know, sir,' said he to me, 'that this is the
very first time in my life, and I am sure in the lives of all
those here present, that we really and actually came into
contact with God's greatest phenomenon of nature, the
greatest genius of music that probably lived on earth?
We are grateful to you, Yehudi's parents!' There was at
this reception also Prof. Sturbe, the one who now oc-
cupies Johann Sebastian Bach's position at the Thomas-
kirche in Leipzig. He said simply: 'This is the greatest
concert I have ever heard in my life!' "

Yehudi can look back to the time when, ill in Brussels,
he was nursed by the Queen of Belgium, the late Queen
Astrid, who treated him as if he were her own child. Or
to the time in Rumania when he practised in the studio

of Enesco before Queen Marie, and she embraced him and autographed one of her own books for him.

Or he can reflect upon his personal contacts with the great figures of music of our day, personal contacts which soon developed into warm friendship—with Sir Edward Elgar, Bruno Walter, Hubay, Respighi, Pizzetti, Enesco.

Which of these many and varied experiences has proved the most thrilling to Yehudi himself? His answer is indicative of his true personality.

"Perhaps I'm sentimental," he has said, "but the most thrilling experience I've ever had was a kiss that maestro Toscanini gave me when he heard me play for the first time. That moment will linger in my memory longer, I think, than any of my successes in Europe and America."

Then, somewhat diffidently (he always talks about himself diffidently), Yehudi will tell you his story.

"I worshipped Toscanini ever since I heard him conduct for the first time. That's why it pained me when I learned that the maestro consistently refused to listen to me play. My former teacher, Adolf Busch—who is a very close friend of Toscanini—begged him to listen to me. But the maestro always closed his eyes with horror, screwed his face with pain, and cried out: 'Prodigies? They all make me sick inside!' It was more than two years of persistent entreaty on the part of Adolph Busch that finally persuaded Toscanini to come to hear me. I did not know that the maestro was in the hall. At the end of the concert, I felt myself suddenly seized and kissed. I looked up, and my heart stood still as I looked into the fiery eyes of the great conductor. He was shouting at me in Italian, at the top of his high-pitched voice. 'You are divine! Yehudi, you are divine! There is no other violinist quite like you!' And ever since that time the maestro and I have been the very best of friends."

Certain phases of the friendship of Toscanini and Yehudi have been widely publicized, such as their trip together on the *Île de France* some years back when Toscanini listened to Yehudi practise for hours. "You know," Toscanini said, when the trip came to a close, "I think I've heard more good music on this trip than I've heard the rest of my life."

The complete story of their friendship has, I believe, never before been told. On one occasion, Yehudi visited the maestro several times at his home in Italy and talked with him about music. One morning, Yehudi said to Toscanini: "Maestro, did you ever hear of the Mozart Seventh Violin Concerto?" "No, *caro* Yehudi," answered Toscanini. "You must be mistaken. Mozart only composed six violin concertos." "But maestro," Yehudi insisted, "Mozart composed seven concertos, and the seventh is probably the most mature and greatest of them all—even though the violinists ignore it." Then Yehudi took out the score, over which maestro Toscanini pored while Yehudi played it for him. In the midst of the slow movement, the telephone rang. Impetuously, Toscanini left his seat, tore the telephone wires out of the wall, then quietly said: "Now, *caro* Yehudi, we can make music without any disturbances!"

In New York City, for weeks at a time, Yehudi and Toscanini would discourse on music at the Astor Hotel. Frequently Yehudi would play for Toscanini, and the maestro would cry out in Italian that the boy played miraculously.

"But maestro," Yehudi once complained with sincerity. "You never correct me when I play. Why don't you tell me when I play badly?"

"There's never anything wrong with your playing, Yehudi," Toscanini answered simply. "It's always perfect."

3

Although several hundred engagements now beckon each year to Yehudi from all corners of the world, he refuses to appear more than fifty times a season—two appearances a week. Four to five months are set aside for concert work. The rest of the time belong to study, rest and a quiet family life. During these months of inactivity,

Yehudi Menuhin

the young Menuhins seclude themselves with Yehudi's parents in Los Gatos, their spacious ranch in California, far removed from people, city life and the garish light of publicity. Here diversions are few and far between. Life is well-ordered and methodical. So many hours each day are devoted to serious study; so many hours belong to the reading of good literature; so many hours are occupied by rest, play and physical exercise—swimming in their private pool, hiking and roaming on the many lonely mountain trails, horseback riding, driving or camping in the enchanting surroundings of the Pacific Coast, or just lounging lazily in the sun.

The Menuhin family is an extraordinary combination of individuals. Time spent in their company is an exhilarating and unforgettable experience. Besides Yehudi, the family consists of two girls, both remarkably talented. Hephzibah has already made her mark as a concert pianist in distinguished sonata recitals with her brother, in extraordinary sonata recordings also with her brother, and in solo appearances. Yaltah, the youngest of the triumvirate, has literary abilities, and has recently even followed Hephzibah's example in making some excellent chamber music recordings with her brother.

In some respects, I think, the Menuhin parents are the most remarkable members of this astonishing family. They were both schoolteachers (neither of them, inci-

259

dentally, is a musician) with excellent cultural back-
grounds. They possess intelligence, tact, and wisdom in
the rearing of children, which is almost an instinct with
them. Raising children is always a precarious task. What,
then, must it be to raise a genius and two extraordinarily
gifted girls? Yet the Menuhins have performed this
difficult task admirably. They balanced their children's
intellectual diet so that it might contain courses other
than music. Moreover, they watched over their physical, as well as mental, development. They never spoiled
the children with excesses of pampering, and they
guarded them carefully from too much praise. As a
result, the three young people today glow with physical
and mental health. Today they are integrated and well-
adjusted personalities.

Yehudi, as a young man, is well developed physically.
He is broad-shouldered, well built, muscular and robust,
alive with health and vitality. His eyes are fresh and
alert; his cheeks, florid and smooth; his body, well disciplined. His mind, moreover, equals the resilience of his
muscles. He speaks and writes in six languages sufficiently
well, reads abundantly in all of these languages. His is
an unusual intellectual curiosity, and a wide intellectual
span. He can discuss art or politics with grace and pene-
tration. As a matter of fact he only rarely discusses music.
I have been at the dinner table of the Menuhins when

the discussion of music was completely absent—politics, social questions or literature being the principal subjects for comment. And in all of these conversations, Yehudi and his sisters indulge freely; and their contributions are often not only pertinent but also strikingly illuminating.

As a personality, Yehudi impressed me most because of his quiet and dignified modesty. Although he is fully aware of his powers as an artist, he remains surprisingly unassuming in the face of this knowledge. He almost never speaks of his successes; and if the conversation inadvertently curves towards a discussion of his achievements, he grows as flustered as a schoolboy who is hearing words of praise. As a boy, he never grumbled at the fact that he must usually be in bed well before midnight, nor did he complain because he never received greater consideration or concessions than his sisters. Today, he is still the well balanced, unspoiled individual. I have never known him to be temperamental or hot-headed. He is equable and completely imperturbable in everyday life as he is on the concert platform. And his complete indifference to money is as charming as it is unusual. He began signing his own checks only after his twenty-first birthday, and only because his father felt that the time had come to give him a feeling of financial responsibility. But his tastes are simple, and he spends his income sparingly. I have spoken to Yehudi many times but not once have I ever heard him measure his success (as so many other artists do) by the yardstick of the box office.

Although he has never played ball—unless ping-pong or badminton are considered ball games—Yehudi is not indifferent to sports. He is enormously fond of swimming. His bicycle was his best friend during his boyhood, and still is. The mountain trails in California often find Yehudi and his wife pedaling for miles. He is passionately fond of motoring. But his greatest delight, particularly when he was younger, is mechanics. Once he was motoring in France when his car broke down suddenly. "Good!" he cried out. "I hope the car's broken. Then I'll have a chance to fix it." He lifted the hood and then, with undisguised glee, went about the task of adjusting the motor. When he finally completed the job, he jumped into the car—dirty-faced, greasy, smudged— and said wistfully: "Too bad it wasn't a harder job!"

4

It should not be necessary to speak in detail of Yehudi's life here, so much of which has already been extensively publicized. A few of the essential facts, however, might not be out of place. He was born in New York on April 22, 1916. A spurious article, published in a national circulation magazine under his mother's name, has questioned his racial origin. But such a question is absurd. Both Yehudi's parents are Jewish. His father, born in Russia and raised in Palestine, was a teacher in Hebrew schools in New York and San Francisco; his mother, though of Tartar extraction on her father's side, has had Jewish antecedents for several generations.

When Yehudi was nine months old, his parents left for San Francisco, where the father was given a position as superintendant of the Jewish Educational Society. In San Francisco Yehudi heard his first concert. He was not a year old, and he had been brought to the concert of the San Francisco Symphony Orchestra only because his parents could not afford the price of a maid. To the amazement of his parents, and those sitting near them, Yehudi was deathly still while the concert was in progress. He was brought to other concerts, and always he seemed to listen with minute and breathless attention.

Those were the first indications he gave of an unusual musical instinct. Another—and a much more forceful one—came when he was three years old. He was given a toy violin, and when he tried it, and discovered that it was spurious, he threw it on the floor in anger.

He received a real violin soon after this incident, and when he had mastered the elements, he performed at a public concert conducted by the Pacific Musical Society of San Francisco. When he was four he received his first lessons from Sigmund Anker; a year and a half later, Louis Persinger—the concert-master of the San Francisco Symphony Orchestra—became his teacher. From that moment on, the playing of the violin ceased to be mere play for Yehudi and became a serious business. His capacity to apply himself to study was extraordinary; he never seemed to grow tired of practising. And he learned with phenomenal rapidity. When he was six, he was ready for concert appearances. He played the Mendelssohn Concerto at the Civic Auditorium in San Francisco before an audience of 9,000—and his playing was nothing short of sensational. His performance, so maturely thought out and so intelligently presented, was publicized throughout the country. A New York engagement was immediately arranged. A few months later, the child gave his historic reading of the Beethoven concerto at the Mecca Temple.

He was not just another prodigy this much was apparent from the very first. It became even more convincingly proved as his career began to unfold. He was a profound artist, with integrity, taste and a high artistic standard to which he clung tenaciously. That he should make his official débuts in San Francisco and New York with two great concertos—those of Mendelssohn and Beethoven—in place of meretricious pieces, was only the first indication that only the highest plane of his art was to be his sphere. This became even more evident in later concerts: when he chose, as his encore, not a fussy trifle, but—on certain occasions—the solo sonatas of Bach; when—as in many of his European appearances—he featured programs consisting of only three major concertos; when (as in the case of the Bach music he played, and the concerto of Paganini) he refused to follow the accepted grooves set out for him by all the violinists before his time, by performing edited versions, but instead went to the original (Urtext) editions and performed the music as the composers had intended it to be performed; when, permitting his vein for experiment full scope, he performed great works of music sometimes rarely, and sometimes never before featured—the *Adelaide Concerto* of Mozart, and the so-called "lost" concerto of Schumann; when he revealed his profound devotion to Bach by never omitting on a concert program either a sonata or a partita by the Leipzig master.

How to explain Yehudi's genius? He seemed to have been born with music within him; an instinctive sixth sense which has frequently proved to be infallible has guided his musical expression. His teachers have often confessed that they have learned as much from him as he from them. Instinctively he has always felt how a certain passage should be performed. Where the interpretation of a phrase, where a nuance, or the moulding of a line are concerned, there was not much that he could be taught. He seemed to have been controlled by forces which none could analyze. Louis Persinger, his first important teacher, once said that at the age of eight Yehudi already had a clear and organized conception of the Beethoven Concerto, and his interpretation in many respects was as integrated as that of many mature artists. It seems that Yehudi's interpretations sprang from an inexhaustible inspiration deep within him. Once it was remarked to Yehudi that on two successive occasions he gave two altogether different interpretations of a Mozart sonata. "What of it?" Yehudi asked with surprise. "I felt the work differently on the second day, and so I played it differently." In words such as these can you find a true artist.

Yehudi has been fortunate to have come under the influence of the great composer, violinist, conductor and teacher, Georges Enesco. Under Enesco, Yehudi's genius ripened maturely. Enesco, Yehudi regards as his greatest friend—and his greatest single influence.

Today, Yehudi combines his instinct, his inspiration, his inborn taste and judgment with maturity, education and disciplined emotions. A combination such as this is always the formula for the production of a truly great musical performance. When we listen to Menuhin play a sonata of Bach or Mozart with the most exquisite sensitivity of tonal design, with an inborn feeling for musical values, and with (at certain moments) a conception that is almost other-worldly, we are tempted to say of him what one critic once said of another great artist: "He is, after all, the greatest artist on his instrument. Because, the way he plays certain things, no one can play anything!"

INDEX

269

INDEX